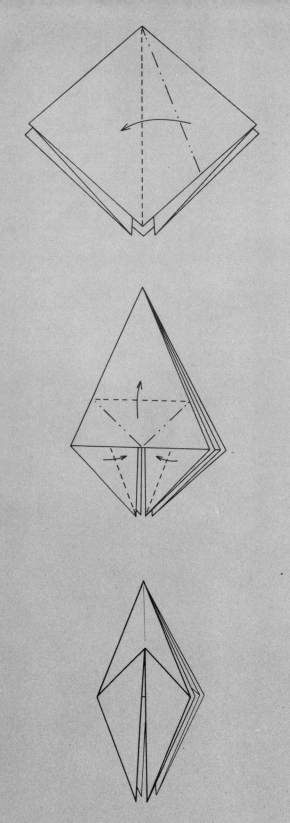

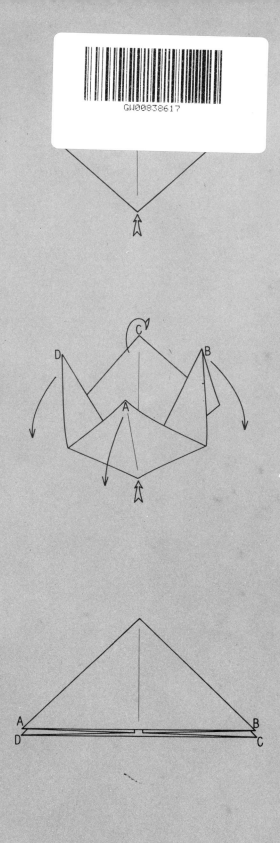

**FROG
BASE**

**WATERBOMB
BASE**

THE BEST OF
OriGaMi

LION by **NEAL ELIAS**, *page 92;* **GIRAFFE** and **ELEPHANT** by **GEORGE RHOADS**, *pages 112 and 134;* **PALM TREE** by **LIGIA MONTOYA**, *page 162.*

THE BEST OF
OriGaMi

NEW MODELS BY CONTEMPORARY FOLDERS

by Samuel Randlett

Line drawings and photographs by Jean Randlett □ Preface by Martin Gardner

FABER AND FABER
3 Queen Square, London W.C.1

First published in England in 1964
by Faber and Faber Limited
3 Queen Square, London, W.C.1
Reprinted 1973
Printed in Great Britain by
Whitstable Litho Ltd, Straker Brothers

ISBN 0 571 10275 1

To Lillian Oppenheimer

CONTENTS

		Page
	Preface	1
	Foreword	3
I.	How to Use This Book: Paper, Tools, Symbols, Procedures, Instructions	4
II.	Introductory Models	14
III.	Diamond Base	41
IV.	Fish Base	49
V.	Preliminary Fold	60
VI.	Bird Base	66
VII.	Bird Base: Stretched Form	96
VIII.	Bird Base: Multiple Forms	108
IX.	Bird Base: Unusual Shapes	118
X.	Blintz Bird Base	126
XI.	Frog Base	140
XII.	Frog Base: Stretched Form	152
XIII.	Frog Base: Hexagonal Sheet	162
XIV.	Waterbomb Base	166
	Contributors	179
	Bibliography	183
	Index	185

ORIGAMI PAPER

Samuel Jones & Co. Ltd., New Bridge Street, London, E.C.4. make a paper suitable for origami which should be available at Boots' stationery departments and at all good stationers as well as handicraft stores. It is called "Butterfly Brand Origami Paper" and will be available in packets of 60 squares of assorted colours.

Colorama paper, mentioned on page 4, is available in rolls 9 ft. wide and in lengths of 12, 25 and 50 yards long. It is marketed by Allied Paper Merchants (W.T.) Ltd., Gateway House, 1, Watling Street, London E.C.4., and is available from large photographic suppliers. This paper is thick, but will crease without cracking, and when used in giant sheets is suitable for making very large models. The heaviness of the paper is advantageous in helping large origami figures to sustain their own weight.

PREFACE

One might suppose that only a limited number of different figures can be folded from that simplest of all art materials, a single sheet of paper. After centuries of paper folding in the Orient, surely (one is tempted to think) the supply of such models must long ago have been exhausted.

Far from it! You have only to flip through the pages of this beautiful book to see quickly that such is not the case. Here are dozens of brand-new folds—charming little replicas of animals, objects, and human figures—constructed with great simplicity, ingenuity, artistic elegance, and delightful humor. By employing Akira Yoshizawa's now widely accepted symbols, and by adopting the terminology recently developed among Western folders, Mr. Randlett has produced one of the most clearly written instruction books on origami in the English language. Mrs. Randlett's superb illustrations leave nothing to be desired. Best of all, Mr. Randlett has drawn upon his vast knowledge of the subject, and his personal acquaintance with many of the Western experts on paper folding, to select for his book the very finest of their new creations.

It is interesting to note, in reading over the valuable biographical sketches in the back of this book, that fully half of the paper folders represented here have made a hobby of conjuring. A common interest in the two arts is perhaps not hard to understand. Both demand considerable finger dexterity; both have entertainment value. Even the great Houdini once wrote a book called *Houdini's Paper Magic* (published in 1922 by Routledge, London and E. P. Dutton & Co., N.Y. Its section on origami contains the first Western book publication of the famous Japanese jumping frog. More recently, Shari Lewis, the daughter of a professional magician and herself one of the world's finest ventriloquists and hand puppeteers, has collaborated with Lillian Oppenheimer on a splendid book about origami action models. I remember attending a magic convention in Chicago in the thirties (yes, magic is my hobby also) at which almost every magician present was wearing a finger ring with a large rectangular "jewel" that he had folded from a dollar bill.

Although magicians have known about paper folding for decades, ten years ago the word "origami" was almost unknown to the general public in this country. Today it is a familiar word. Thousands of people, of all ages and walks of life, have discovered the pleasures of this fascinating, gentle art. Why has it so strongly caught the fancy of the Western people? The causes are no doubt varied and complex, but if I were asked to name the single, most effective cause, I would answer unhesitatingly: Lillian Oppenheimer.

It was Mrs. Oppenheimer who started the Origami Center in New York City, the first organized attempt to teach the art to Westerners. It was she who started *The Origamian,* the first periodical ever devoted to the art. It was she who traveled around the world, seeking out the leading paper folders, putting them in touch with one another, stimulating them to work on new constructions. It was she who worked (in 1959) with The Cooper Union Museum for the Arts of Decoration on the first U.S. exhibit of paper folding. This book, appropriately dedicated to Lillian Oppenheimer, is a splendid tribute to her pioneer efforts and boundless enthusiasm.

Let me close with a little fable. The scene is a cocktail party in a New York suburb. Someone has just folded a flapping crane for the host's little girl. She is transported with delight. In a far corner of the room a man shakes his head and mutters to the lady next to him: "Isn't it amazing the lengths to which people will go to find ways of wasting their time?" Comes Monday morning. The man who folded the bird goes to his office; he is a surgeon specializing in lung ailments. The man who scoffed at paper folding reports to work at a large advertising agency. There he spends the week devising a brilliant new format for a TV cigarette commercial.

Martin Gardner

FOREWORD

Origami is the only branch of sculpture that is, like music, a performance art; an origami figure exists in diagrams, as a string quartet exists in a musical score. Part of the charm of this little art lies here, for in "performing" a paper model, we share the joy of the creative artist. We *look* at a statue that a sculptor has carved from stone, but we *make* an origami figure, actively following its evolution from a piece of paper into a bird, an animal, or a useful object.

The Best of Origami, then, is a sort of sculpture exhibition in print—a display case for new models. Each of the traditional *basic folds* (the simple geometrical foundations of origami) has a chapter to itself; the section on the Bird Base and its variants is the most comprehensive survey of a single basic fold yet to be published. Within each chapter the models are presented in order of difficulty, proceeding gradually from elementary figures to the heights of origami virtuosity. The book should therefore be equally well suited to the needs of the beginner and the more advanced folder.

Western folders have not been contented merely to assimilate the Oriental tradition: they have gone on to develop the potentialities of the medium in a most impressive way. A great variety of styles and subjects will be found here; the human figure, neglected in the Orient during recent decades, is well represented, and there are several brilliant solutions to the problem of combining two subjects in a single model. Many of the figures begin with the conventional square of paper; others are folded from triangles, rectangles, diamond shapes, or hexagons. Each model embodies some novelty of concept or technique.

It is a pleasure to thank the contributors to this anthology, whose generosity in making their creations available for inclusion was matched only by their kind assistance during its production. Special thanks must be given to Neal Elias, whose notebooks made the task of selection and organization simpler than it would otherwise have been, and to Robert Harbin, whose cooperation has made it possible for the present volume and his own excellent origami anthology to be mutually complementary.

Samuel Randlett

Wilmette, Illinois
March, 1963

I. HOW TO USE THIS BOOK

PAPER

Thin crisp paper that will take a sharp crease is best. *Origami paper*, made in Japan especially for folding, is ideal for most small models. It comes in a variety of hues and figured patterns, brightly colored on one side and white on the other. The largest sheet usually available is seven inches square. Origami paper can be inexpensively obtained from Japanese importers.

Other types of paper are suitable, however. *Gift-wrap* papers are available in dozens of patterns and colors at any stationery store, and can be had in metallic finishes. Most of these papers are excellent for folding. Some sorts of *shelf paper* are satisfactory. The test is how well the particular paper can be creased.

Some models need paper colored on both sides. Ordinary brown *wrapping paper* is strong, and good for large exhibition models that have to withstand a certain amount of wear. It can be tinted with any shade of ink; but a host of department stores use wrapping papers and bags of several different colors: green, blue, gray, and the darker shades of red are common. Dry cleaners' bags should not be overlooked as a convenient source of large sheets. *Typing paper* (bond) comes in many pastel shades used for mimeograph work; the lighter weights are satisfactory for origami.

Paper for big models can be thicker. *Pastel paper* comes in several shades; *velour paper* has a furry surface. (Both are sold by art stores.) *Wallpaper* tends to crack, but there are a few relatively thin types, including wood-grained patterns. *Day-glo* is fluorescent paper, brilliantly colored. *Poster paper*, easily obtained from art and school supply stores, is not crisp enough for intricate models, but it can be used for simple figures with few folds. *Colorama* is seamless paper three yards wide, available in many colors from photography stores.

Waxed paper, *tissue paper*, and translucent *tracing paper* are worth experimenting with for an occasional special effect.

TOOLS

A paper cutter is extremely useful for squaring. Twelve inches is the smallest practical size; you will want a bigger one if you make many large models for exhibition. (Paper cutters are sold by office equipment stores and—as print trimmers—by photographic supply houses.)

Paper can, however, be squared with a scissors or a knife:

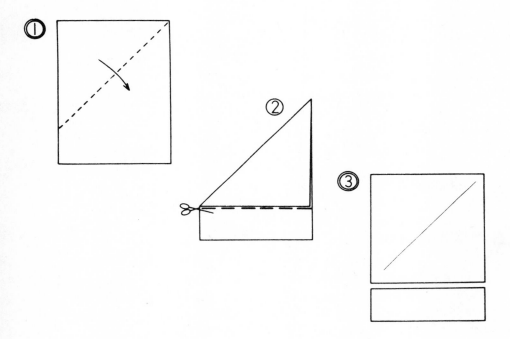

In addition to a paper cutter or a large pair of scissors, you will need a small, straight, sharp scissors for work on details. (Sharp pointed $4\frac{1}{2}$ in. is a good size.) A razor blade or X-acto knife is occasionally helpful. Cuts are sometimes used in origami models, but the effect must be strong enough to justify this liberty.

Cellophane tape is suggested in several places as an aid to understanding the structure of some of the more intricate double bases. All such bases are properly folded from untaped sheets; the tape is to be used only for purposes of learning.

A piece of Masonite about a foot square makes a convenient surface for folding.

SYMBOLS

Valley fold $\quad$ -

Mountain fold $\quad$ — · — · · — · · — · — · · — · — · · — · ·

Cut $\quad$ — — — — — — — — — — — — ⟶✄

Existing crease $\quad$ ————————————————

Previous position
  (or X-ray view) $\quad$ ·

Hold here $\quad$ ○

Watch this spot $\quad$ ✕

In front

Behind

Tuck in; or
  open out; or
  apply force

Fold over and over

Turn model over

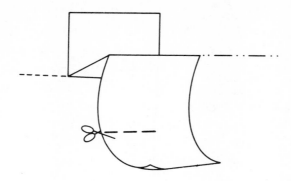

SYMBOLS

Akira Yoshizawa's code of lines and arrows, shown at the left, is rapidly becoming the international language of the origami world. It is used throughout this book.

A series of dashes represents a *valley fold*. Make a concave crease wherever such a line appears in the illustrations.

A series of dots and dashes is a *mountain fold,* indicating a convex crease.

Heavy dashes with a tiny pair of scissors indicate a *cut.*

Notice the different types of arrow. The interpretation of the hollow fork-tailed arrow depends on its context; the other arrows have fixed and invariable meanings.

FOLLOWING THE INSTRUCTIONS

1. All but a few models are made from squares.
2. The first drawing of each model has a double ring around its number. The drawing of the completed model is similarly identified.
3. The colored side of the paper is showing in fig. 1 of each model. Exceptions are always noted in the text.
4. The model is always drawn as it will look at the *beginning* of a particular step. The folds to be made are shown by the lines and arrows, and described one by one in the text. Look ahead to the illustration of the *next* step to see where you are going. Follow both the drawings and the text; the drawings are not always complete in themselves.
5. Flaps are named for their points; thus "flap A" is the flap with the letter "A" at its point. Lettering is consistent for any given model; flap A remains flap A until the model is complete.

6. All words having to do with direction—*up, down, right, left, in front, behind,* etc.—are to be understood with regard to the page itself. "Fold upward" thus means "fold toward the top of the page." "Forward" is toward you, "behind" is away from you, and so forth.

7. Valley folds are more common than mountain folds. Therefore the verb "fold" when not otherwise qualified is to be understood as meaning "valley-fold." Mountain folds are always called mountain folds.

8. Because most models are symmetrical, folds made in front are often repeated on the back of the model. The standard instruction for this is "repeat behind," which means to repeat on the far side only.

9. Each section of the book consists of models derived from a single basic fold. All of the models made from the Diamond Base, for instance, are grouped together. Within each section, the models are arranged in approximate order of difficulty. The last models in one section are more difficult than the first models in the next section.

10. Any model will be easier to fold if you concentrate on the drawings while someone else reads the instructions to you. It is also possible to label the points of your model with penciled letters like those of the drawings.

11. Make a sample of each basic fold as you come to it—Diamond Base, Fish Base, etc.—and keep the sample handy for reference. This will save thumbing through the pages to find instructions. An abbreviated chart of some of the more common bases is included at the end of the book.

PROCEDURES

Several common procedures isolated and named by Robert Harbin are shown below in detail. Refer back to these pages whenever necessary.

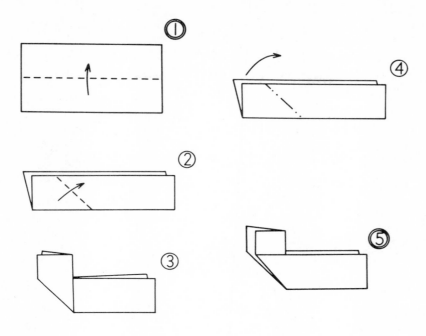

Reverse Fold

1. Bring the bottom edge to the top and crease to form a trough.
2. Valley-fold the doubled paper upward in front, in preparation for the reverse fold to follow. (Note that the arrow for a valley fold *crosses* the line.)
3. Return the paper to its former position.
4. To make the reverse fold, push upward on the left end of the bottom crease, bringing it up *between* the two sides of the trough. The crease will reverse itself. (Note that the arrow for a reverse fold does *not* cross the line.)
5. The reverse fold is complete. A reverse fold may be made at any angle, but it will always fold a trough into or around itself. In this example the trough was folded into itself.

The reverse fold shown below folds the trough around itself.

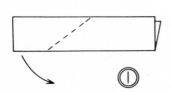

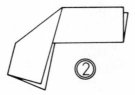

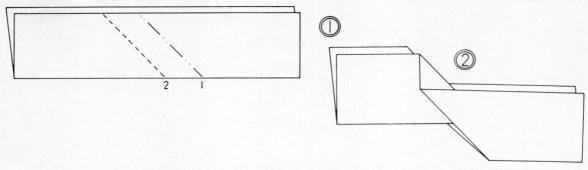

Two reverse folds are often shown in one drawing, as in fig. 1 above. Form each of the two reverse folds separately.

Lovers' Knot Move

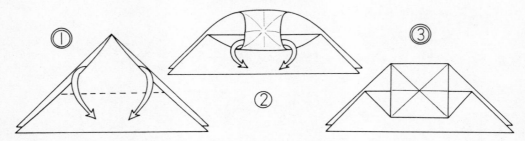

Pull the near upper edges toward yourself and down in a sort of hinge action so that the point will flatten itself. (The classical example of this procedure is the traditional Lovers' Knot.)

Sinking a Point

A point is sunken by pushing it into the model. It is often easiest to open the model out flat, make the necessary mountain-creases, and return the model to its original position.

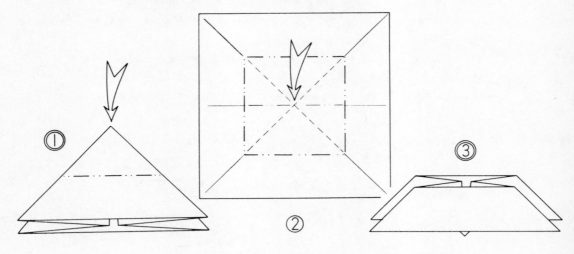

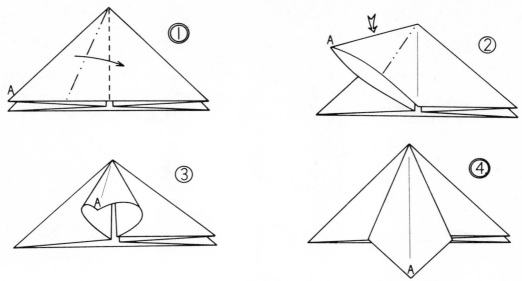

Squash Fold

1. The standard notation of the squash fold is shown in fig. 1. To make the squash fold, begin by lifting flap A.
2. Squash flap A downward, opening out its two sides.
3. The action is shown here in progress.
4. The squash fold is complete.

Petal Fold

1. A petal fold is always preceded by a squash fold. The standard notation of a petal fold is shown in fig. 1. Begin by lifting point A up toward point B.
2. Bring the raw edges of flap A together along the center line, and flatten A so that its tip touches point B.
3. The petal fold is finished.

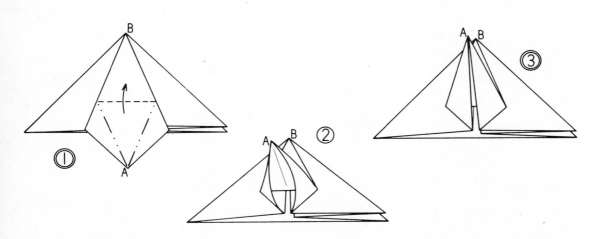

11

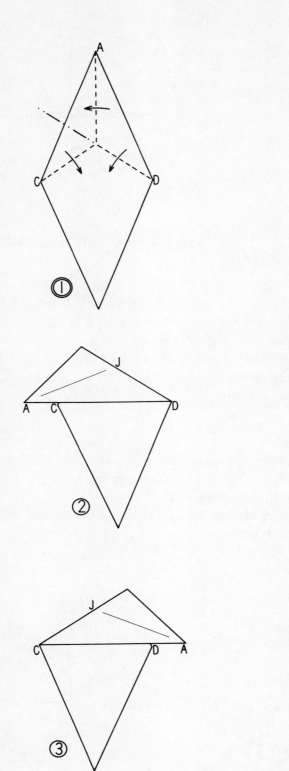

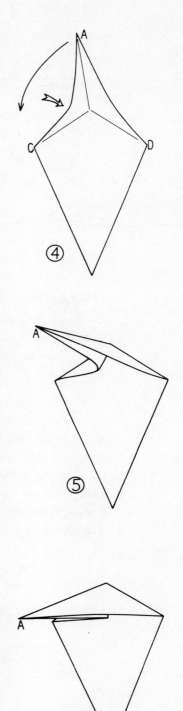

1. The standard notation of a rabbit-ear is shown in fig. 1. Begin by folding side AD over to the left so that it touches point C.
2. Crease from D to J. Return the paper to its former position, and bring side AC over to the right so that it touches point D.
3. Crease from D to J. Lift flap A and pinch its sides together along the center line AJ.
4. Flatten flap A to the left with its sides still pinched together.
5. The action is shown here in progress.
6. The rabbit-ear is complete. A rabbit-ear is always made from a triangular area of the paper—in this case ACD—by creases that bisect the angles of the triangle.

Book Fold

A book fold is a central crease parallel to the edges of the paper. The term is extended to include leafing over the flaps of a model like the pages of a book.

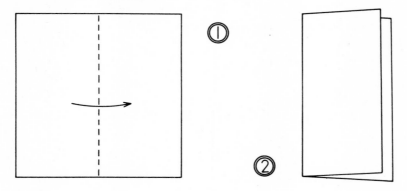

Crimp

This procedure is often used to form heads.

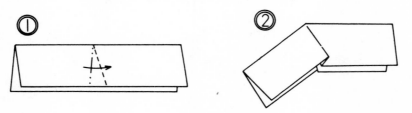

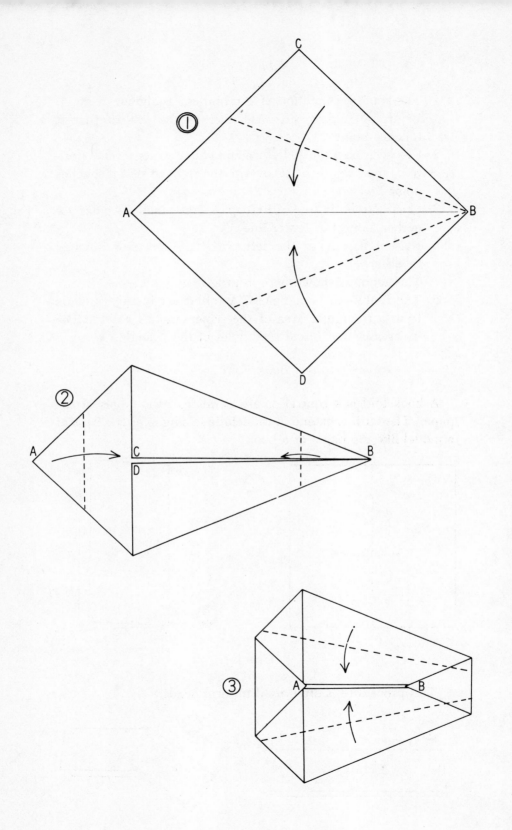

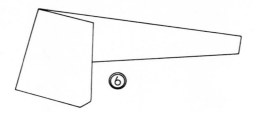

II. INTRODUCTORY MODELS

HATCHET *by Florence Temko*

Begin with a square of paper. The white side of the paper should face you.

1. Fold edges CB and DB to the center line.
2. Fold the tip of flap A to the right so that it barely overlaps C and D. Fold B to the left.
3. Bring the upper and lower edges together along the center line.
4. Fold the model in half.
5. Crimp the left end of the model downward to form the blade of the Hatchet.
6. The Hatchet, which makes a good party favor, holds its shape best when made of metallic paper.

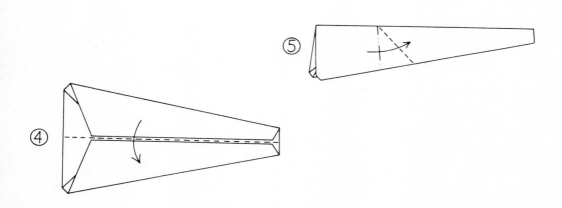

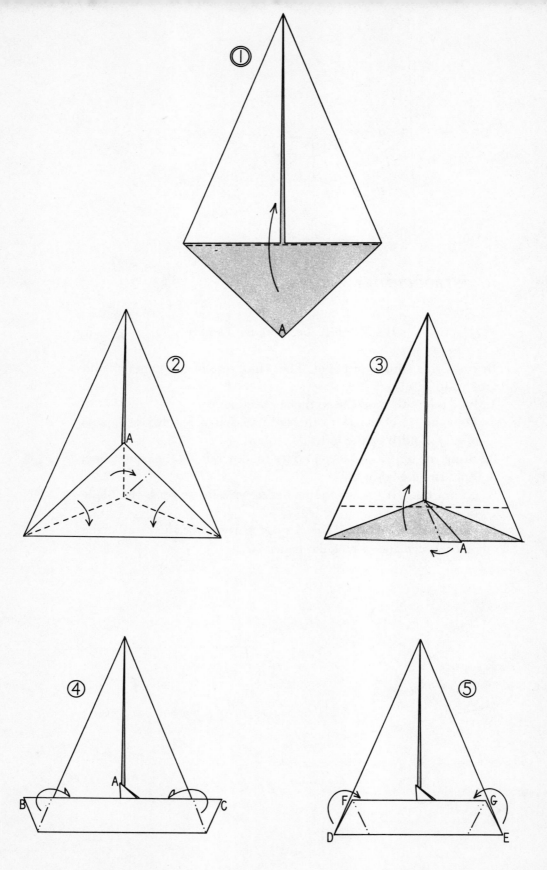

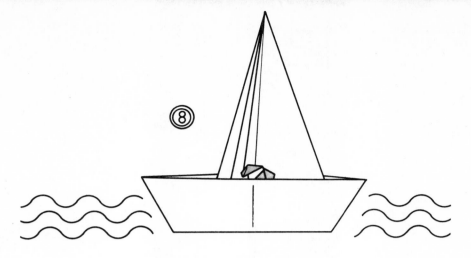

MAN IN A BOAT *by Robert Harbin*

Proceed through step 1 of the Hatchet, page 14. Rotate the model to the position shown here.

1. Fold flap A upward.
2. Form a rabbit-ear of flap A.
3. Reverse-fold the tip of flap A to the left. Fold the bottom edge of the model upward—note the position of this fold.
4. Mountain-fold corners B and C, tucking them between the front and back halves of the model.
5. Reverse-fold corners D and E upward so that points D and E lie just below line FG.
6. Tuck the sail down into the boat like the flap of an envelope; the flap will cover points D and E inside the boat. Reverse-fold the tip of flap A to form the sailor's hat.
7. Form the mast by pleating the sail with the valley fold and mountain fold shown. Complete the sailor by folding his near right edge to the left.
8. Robert Harbin makes this model as shown here, with the sailboat white and only the tiny sailor's cap and jacket colored.

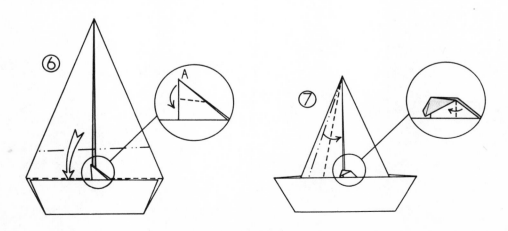

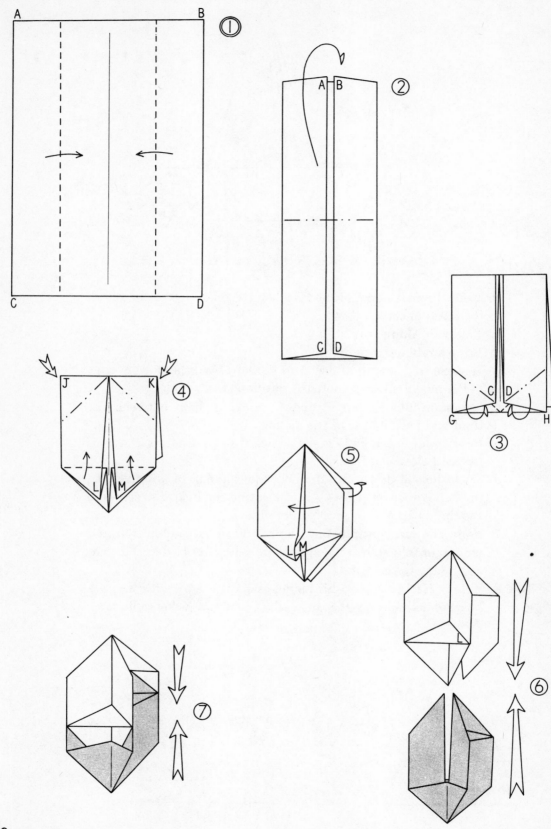

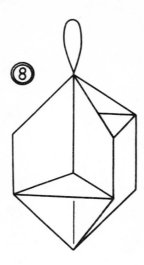

ORNAMENT   *by John M. Nordquist*

Begin with a two-by-three rectangle. The white side of the paper should face you.

1. Fold the edges to the center line.
2. Mountain-fold the model in half.
3. Reverse-fold the corners up so that G and H lie on the center line. Repeat behind.
4. Fold flaps L and M upward. Repeat behind. Reverse-fold the upper corners downward so that J and K lie on the center line.
5. Arrange flaps L and M so that they point toward you. Open flap L and insert flap M into it, swinging the right front edge of the model to the left until flap L completely covers flap M. Repeat behind.
6. Proceed through step 5 with a second two-by-one rectangle of the same size. Turn this duplicate model upside down and revolve it to the position shown here.
7. The two halves of the Ornament are shown here in the process of being pushed together. The points of the upper half must be hidden inside the pockets of the lower half, and vice versa. (The action is facilitated if the pockets are opened out.)
8. The Ornament is especially striking when made from two different colors of metallic paper. See page 109 for a photograph.

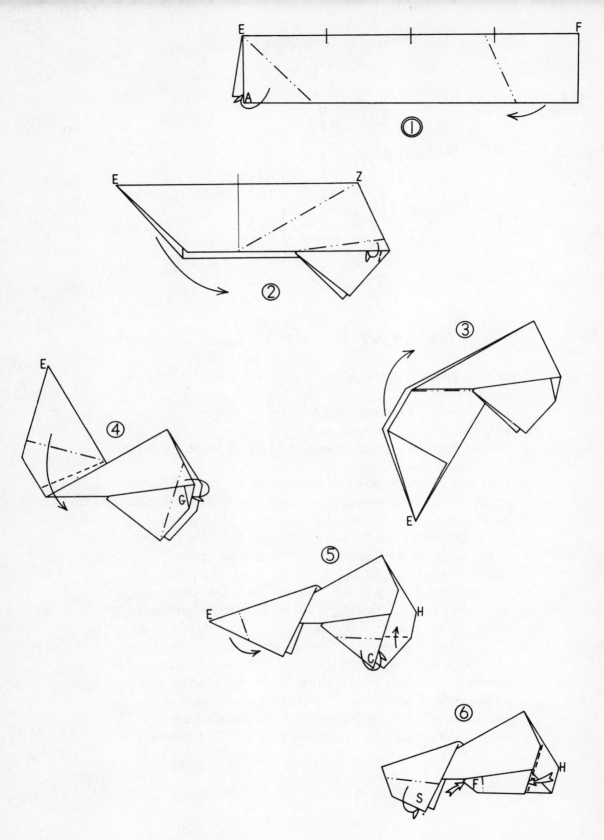

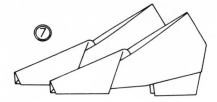

SHOE *by Neal Elias*

Begin with a dollar bill or any other three-by-seven rectangle. Fold the paper in half.

1. Mountain-fold corner A inward so that AE lies along EF. Repeat behind. Then reverse-fold F to the left. (Edge EF is divided into quarters by the vertical strokes to help in the accurate location of this reverse fold.)

2. Reverse-fold E down and to the right. (Edge EZ is divided into halves by the vertical line to locate this reverse fold accurately.) Tuck in the lower edge of the model at the right; repeat behind.

3. Reverse-fold flap E upward.

4. Crimp flap E downward. Mountain-fold area G into the model.

5. Reverse-fold the tip of E into the model. Mountain-fold area C up into the model; repeat behind.

6. Mountain-fold area S up into the shoe. Repeat behind. Reverse-fold corner F to the right. Fold flap H into the model, interlocking it with flap C (see fig. 5) to hold the heel together.

7. For informal entertainment, a dollar bill can be converted into the Shoe to show that money not only talks but walks.

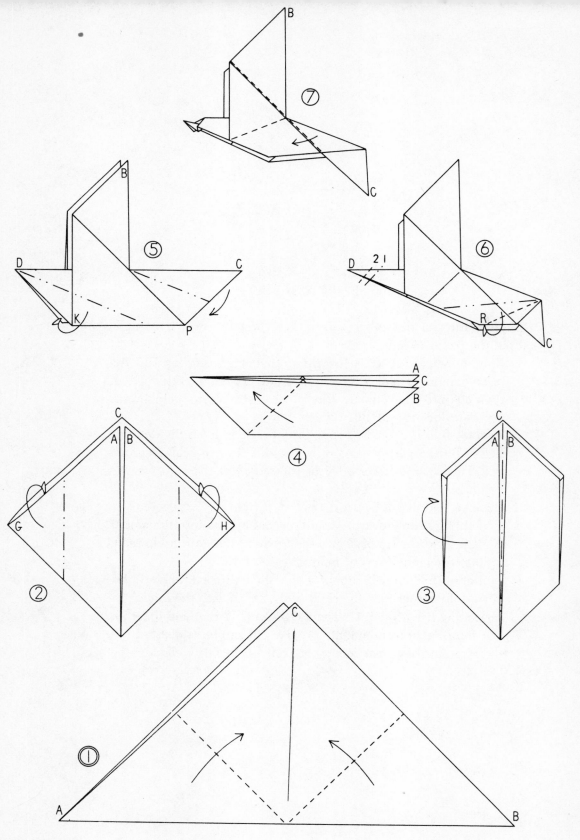

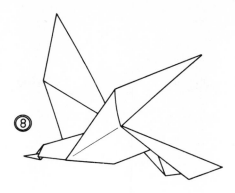

EAGLE *by Samuel Randlett*

Begin with a square folded in half diagonally.
1. Fold points A and B up to point C.
2. Tuck G in between flaps A and C so that its tip touches the midpoint of the center line. Repeat with H.
3. Mountain-fold the model in half, and rotate it to the position shown in fig. 4.
4. Fold flap B up as far as possible. Repeat behind.
5. Mountain-fold flap K into the model so that edge DK lies along line DC. Repeat behind. Reverse-fold flap C downward so that it touches point P.
6. Make in order the two reverse folds indicated on flap D. Tuck area R up into the model as shown; repeat behind.
7. Fold the front half of tail C down around the body. Repeat behind. Form in wing B the two indicated valley-creases. Shape the other wing similarly.
8. The Eagle's wings should stand out from the body in flying position.

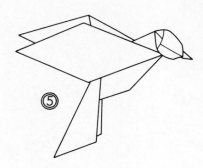

SONGBIRD *by Samuel Randlett*

1. Proceed through step 5 of the Eagle, page 22. Crimp flap D downward. Fold wing B down; repeat behind. Tuck area R up into the model as shown; repeat behind. (Note that the angle of this fold is slightly different from the angle in step 6 of the Eagle.)
2. Open out and fold down the near layer of the head. Repeat behind.
3. Form in order the two reverse folds shown. Roll the lower edge of the head inward; repeat behind. Adjust the edge upward at the right as indicated by the hollow arrow; repeat behind.
4. Narrow the front of the beak with a mountain fold. Repeat behind. Sink the top of the head.
5. The Songbird's tail is folded down around the body as in step 7 of the Eagle.

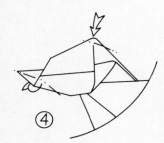

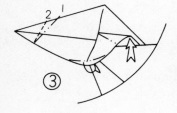

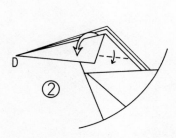

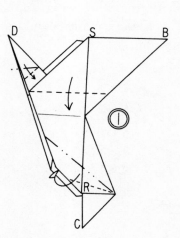

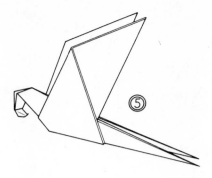

PARROT *by Samuel Randlett*

1. Proceed through step 4 of the Eagle, page 22. Mountain-fold area R up into the model so that edge CR lies along line CD. Repeat behind. Then treat area K similarly. Repeat behind.
2. Reverse-fold D down to begin formation of the head. Narrow flap C again, in front and in back. Then slit the top edge of the model from point C to the wings.
3. This is a close-up view of the head. Reverse-fold D to the right.
4. Open out the inner layers of the beak, and reverse-fold its tip.
5. Compare the Parrot with the Eagle and the Songbird.

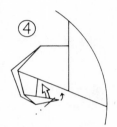

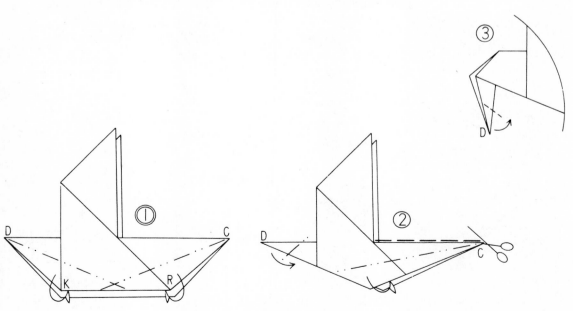

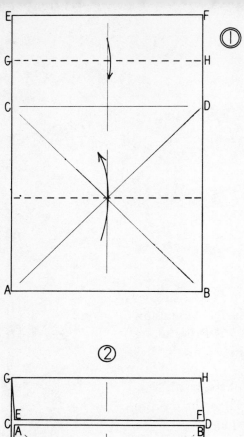

①

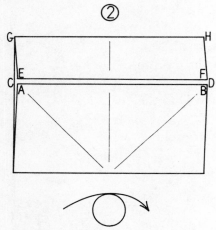

②

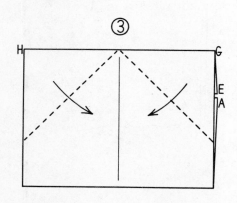

③

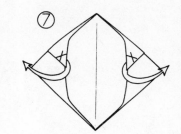

④

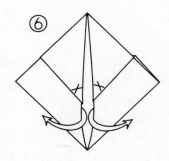

⑤

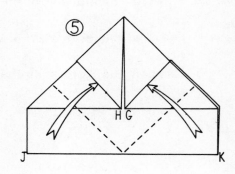

⑥

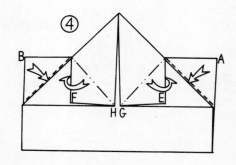

⑦

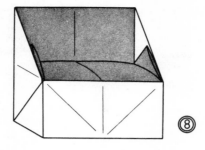

SOFA *by Adolfo Cerceda*

Begin with a two-by-three rectangle.

1. The area ACDB is square. Fold edge AB up to line CD. Fold edge EF down to line CD.
2. Turn the model over.
3. Fold the upper corners downward so that points H and G lie on the center line.
4. Fold corners B and A down so that they lie between the front and back halves of the model. Mountain-fold corners F and E (each a single layer) up into the pockets that lie above them, so that they touch the center line.
5. Fold corners J and K up into the same pockets, so that they touch the center line.
6. Hook your thumbs into the central slit, and pull your hands apart. Watch the spots marked X.
7. We are looking at the bottom rim of the Sofa. Continue pulling until this rim assumes a rectangular shape; then pinch the rounded contours into sharp creases. Set the Sofa upright so that it looks like fig. 8.
8. It is possible to make a chair with the same structure as the Sofa, though the method of folding must be quite different.

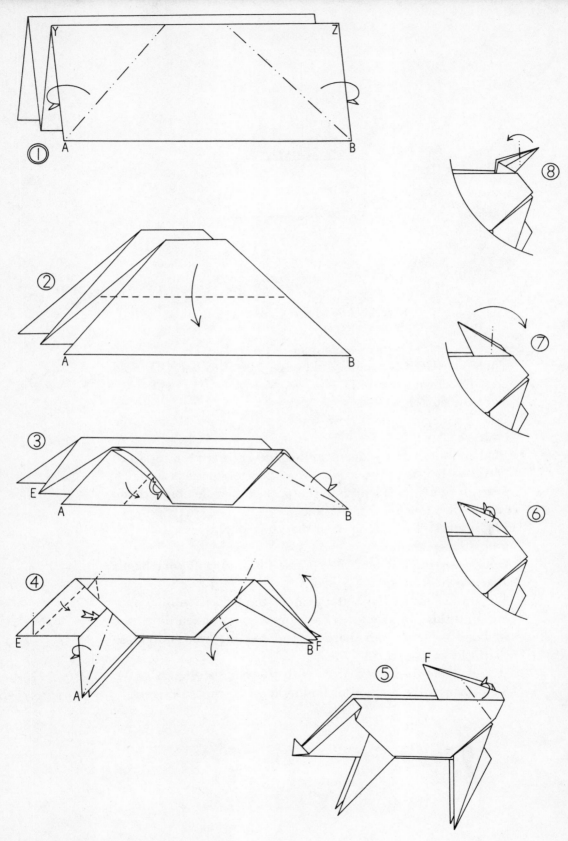

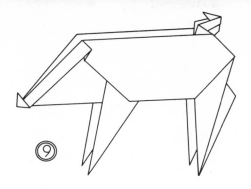

PIGLET *by George Rhoads*

Begin with a five-by-eight rectangle. Fold it as shown in fig. 1; note that AB is the shorter side of the rectangle.

1. Reverse-fold the upper corners so that AY and BZ lie along AB. Repeat behind.
2. Fold the top edge down to the bottom edge. Repeat behind.
3. Fold flap A down into the position shown in fig. 4. Repeat behind. Mountain-fold flap B in the "natural" way (which is not quite in half). Repeat behind.
4. Fold flap B downward; repeat behind. Reverse-fold F upward a little farther than it will comfortably go. Mountain-fold A in half; repeat behind. Fold the upper edge of flap E downward; repeat behind. The tip of E will rise to form the snout.
5. Begin narrowing tail F.
6. Continue to narrow the tail.
7. Reverse-fold the tail to the right.
8. Reverse-fold the tip of the tail to the left again.
9. Note the economy with which the Piglet is folded.

PIGLETS by GEORGE RHOADS, with HOG by SAMUEL RANDLETT,
page 148.

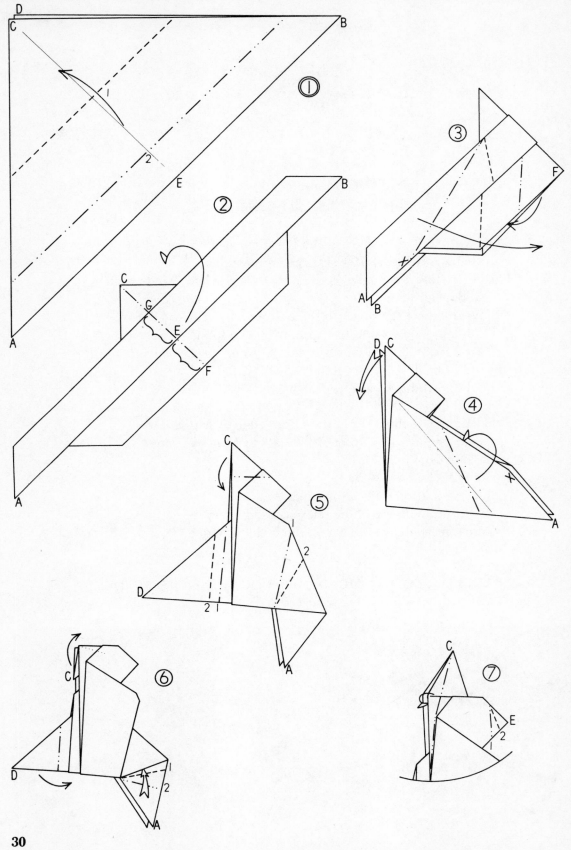

30

INDIAN *by Neal Elias*

Begin with a square of paper folded in half diagonally.

1. Fold edge AEB up so that E touches C, forming valley fold 1. Then fold edge AEB back down again so that distances EG and EF in fig. 2 are equal.

2. Mountain-fold the model in half.

3. Reverse-fold F into the model. Then lift flap A and swing it to the right, flattening it into the position shown in fig. 4 in a sort of squash fold.

4. Loosen the single corner marked D and pull it down to the left as far as it will go. Then mountain-fold flap A into the model; repeat behind.

5. Reverse-fold C downward. Make in order the two reverse folds indicated on flap D. Then form mountain fold 1 and valley fold 2 in flap A; repeat behind.

6. Reverse-fold C upward to form the feather. Reverse-fold flap D into the model. Then form valley fold 1 in flap A, and tuck mountain fold 2 up into the model as indicated by the hollow arrow; repeat behind.

7. Narrow the feather and the spine. Then form in order the two reverse folds indicated in flap E.

8. It is possible to vary the proportions of the Indian by altering the positions of the creases in steps 1 and 3.

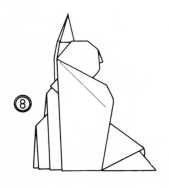

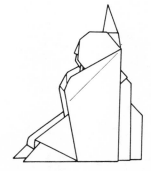

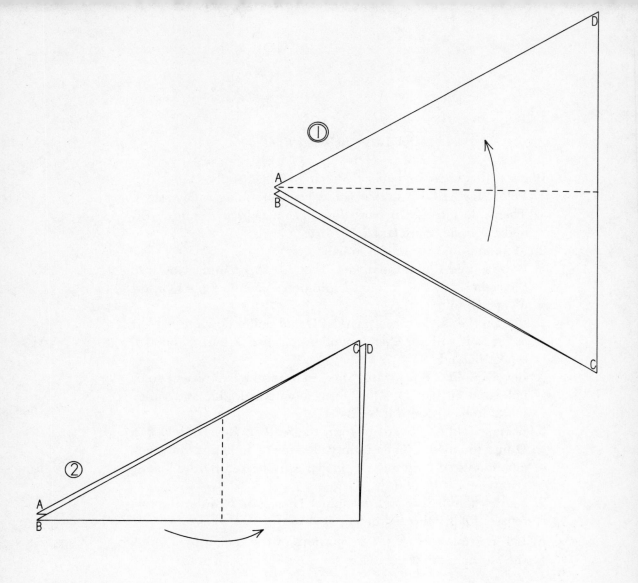

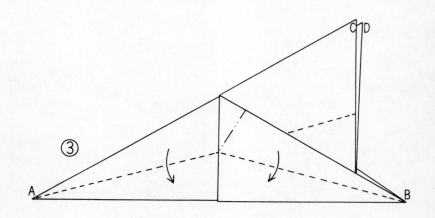

32

STORK *by Ligia Montoya*

Begin with a diamond-shaped piece of paper, folded in half as shown in fig. 1. (ACD, the front half of the paper in fig. 1, is an equilateral triangle: each of its angles equals sixty degrees. A sixty-degree angle may be folded by trisecting the straight edge of a piece of paper; a protractor or a draftsman's 30–60-degree triangle may, however, be used.)

1. Valley-fold the model in half.
2. Reverse-fold flap B (a single layer) to the right.
3. Fold the upper edge AC down to the bottom, and fold the upper edge of flap B to the bottom simultaneously, working from its tip. Repeat behind.
4. (The tip of flap B should now touch the tip of flap C. If it does not, adjust the position of the reverse fold in fig. 2.) Reverse-fold flap A upward. Note the position of this reverse fold on the bottom edge of the model.

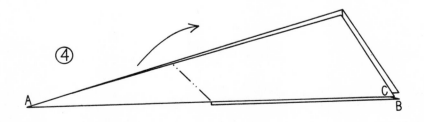

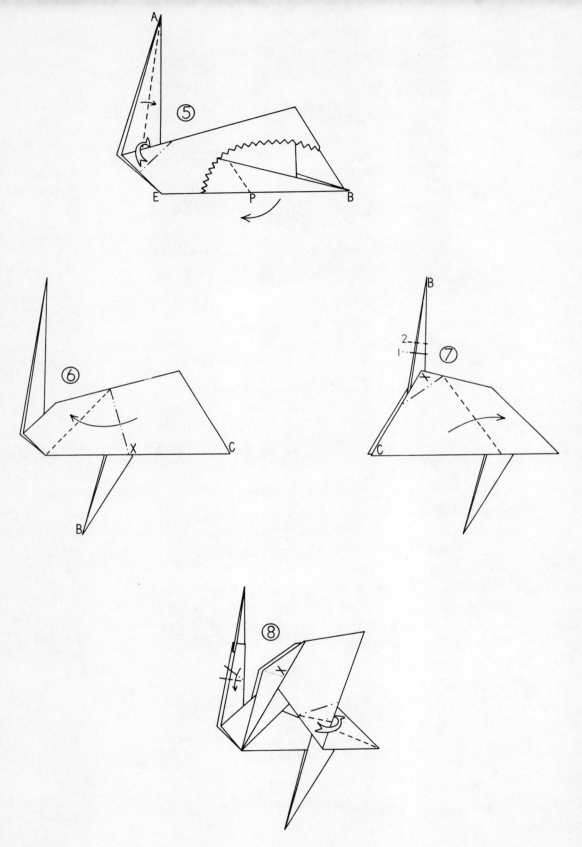

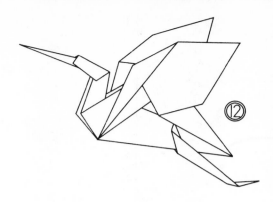

5. Working from its tip, narrow neck A in front and behind. (The front of the model is torn away in the drawing, to show flap B.) Reverse-fold B downward. Note that point P lies halfway between E and B.

6. Lift flap C and swing it to the left in a sort of squash fold. Watch the spot marked X. Repeat behind.

7. Lift wing C and flatten it up and to the right. Watch the spot marked X. Repeat behind. Make in order the two reverse folds shown on flap B.

8. Crimp the head down. Tuck the tail area between wing and body as indicated by the hollow arrow; repeat behind.

9. Reverse-fold the leg to the right.

10. Narrow the leg by sinking its lower edge upward.

11. Form a foot by reverse-folding the tip of the leg.

12. Miss Montoya has used this procedure to make several other fine birds.

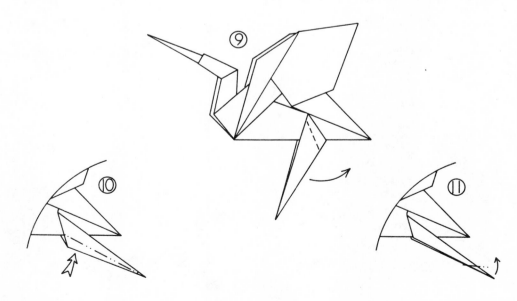

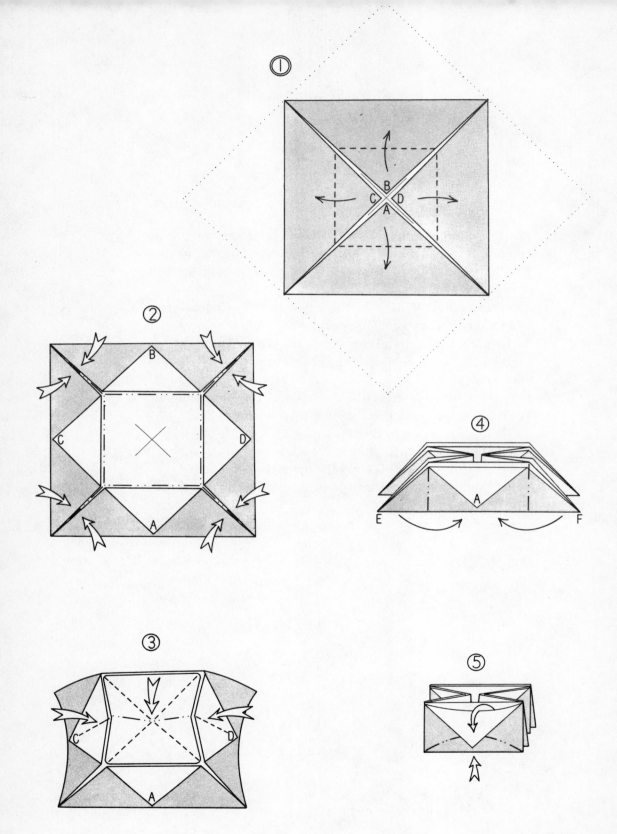

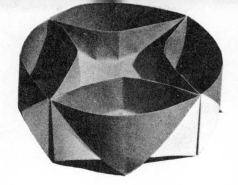

LAZY SUSAN (*Traditional Chinese*)

Fold the four corners of a square to the center. (The dotted lines in fig. 1 show the outline of the flat sheet.)

1. Fold each flap out so that it touches the edge of the model.
2. Pinch each corner of the model to produce the mountain folds shown. Form a mountain fold running inside the border of the central square area.
3. Sink the central square area down into the model, applying pressure at the same time on sides C and D to bring the model to the configuration shown in fig. 4.
4. Reverse-fold corners E and F into the model. Repeat behind.
5. Insert your finger down into the front pocket and pull toward yourself. Push up on the bottom of the pocket at the same time, forming a curved crease in its front and back surfaces. Repeat behind and on the sides.
6. This is a top view of the Lazy Susan. Sharpen the creases of the central compartment.
7. The Lazy Susan is a figure traditional in the Szechwan province of west China; its five compartments represent the five happinesses. (Five is a lucky number to the Chinese.) Mr. Chris Chow introduced the model to America by teaching it to Mr. Philip Shen, who popularized the model among devotees of origami.

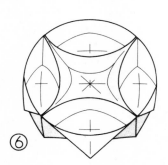

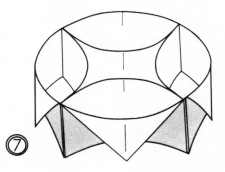

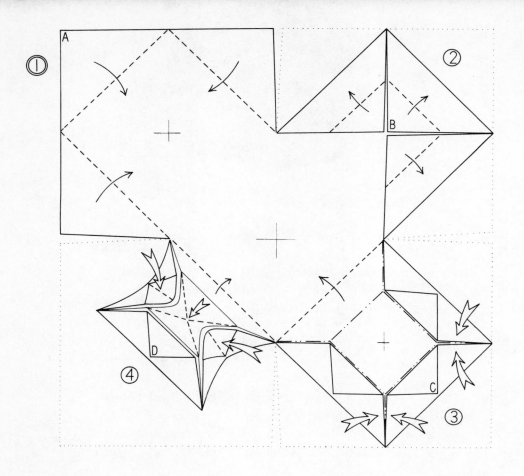

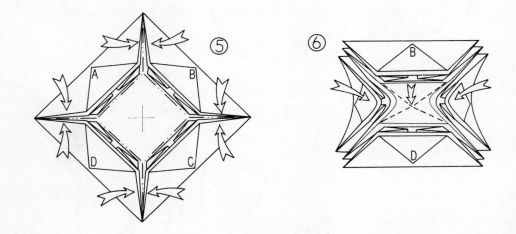

38

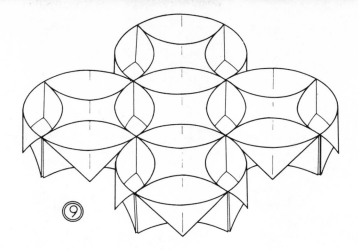

⑨

SUPER SUSAN *by John M. Nordquist*

This figure consists of five interlocked Lazy Susans. Be sure that you understand the folding of the Lazy Susan before attempting the Super Susan. Begin with a large square of paper, as indicated by the dotted line. Slit the middle of each side exactly halfway to the center of the paper. Figs. 1 through 4 show the steps through which each of the four resulting flaps must go.

1. Fold the three free corners to the center of the flap.
2. Fold the corners out again.
3. Pinch each corner and mountain-fold the central square. Fold the entire flap toward the center of the large sheet.
4. Sink the central square, applying pressure to the sides.

Repeat steps 1 through 4 with each of the four flaps.

5. Pinch each corner and mountain-fold the central square.
6. Sink the central square, applying pressure to the sides.
7. Reverse-fold all twelve corners into the model.
8. Open out each of the twenty-one pockets.
9. The Super Susan is a fine example of logic as a creative element in origami.

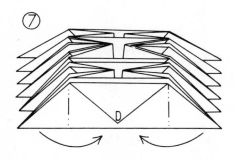

⑦

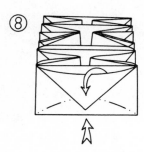

⑧

PARROTS by SAMUEL RANDLETT, *page 25;* FLAMINGO by ADOLFO
CERCEDA, *page 156;* PALM TREE by LIGIA MONTOYA, *page 162;* SPIDER
MONKEY by NEAL ELIAS, *page 116.*

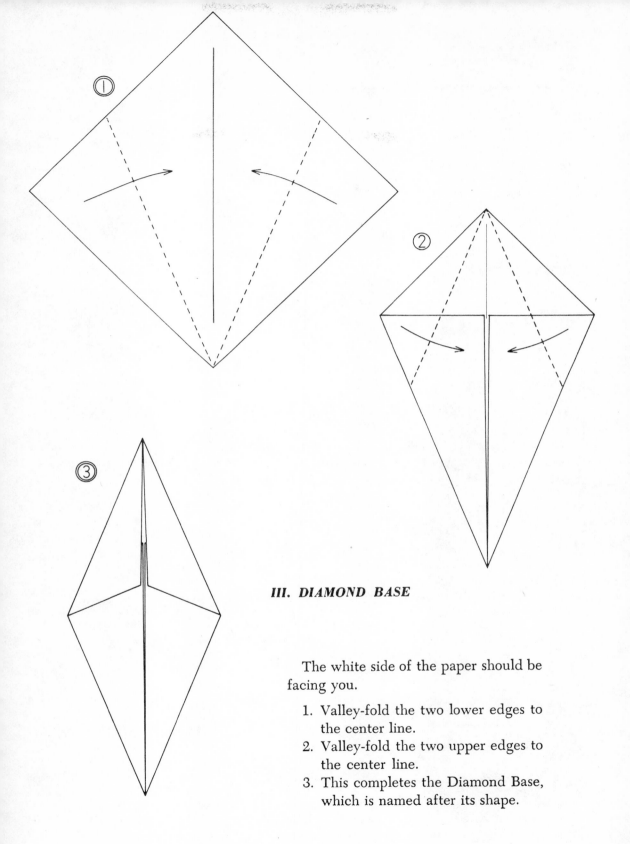

III. DIAMOND BASE

The white side of the paper should be facing you.

1. Valley-fold the two lower edges to the center line.
2. Valley-fold the two upper edges to the center line.
3. This completes the Diamond Base, which is named after its shape.

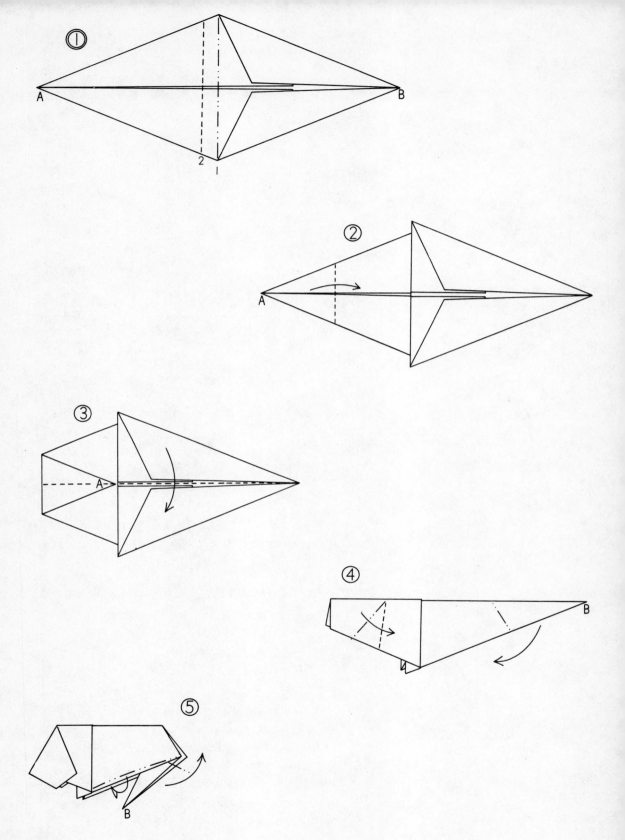

42

THURBER DOG *by Robert Neale*

Begin with the Diamond Base, page 41.

1. Mountain-fold flap A to the right, so that its tip touches point B. Then fold it to the left again, leaving a collar in back.
2. Fold the tip of flap A to the right.
3. Fold the model in half.
4. Crimp the head downward. Reverse-fold flap B downward.
5. Reverse-fold flap B up again to form the hind legs and tail. Mountain-fold the lower edge of the model inward slightly; repeat behind.
6. This is a good model for teaching purposes. By changing the size of the head, the Thurber Dog may be made into a Scottie.

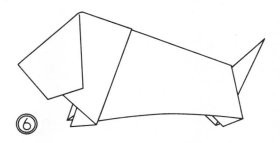

⑥

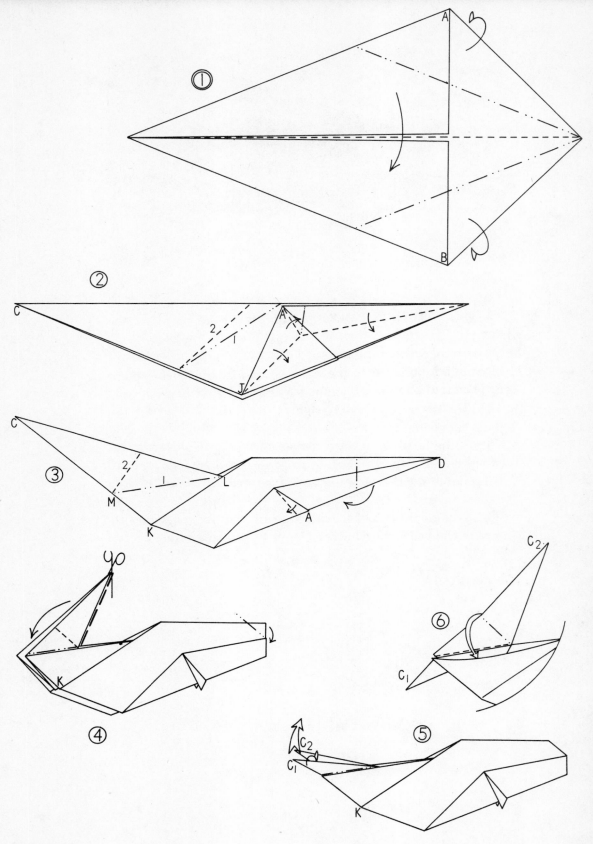

WHALE *by Robert Neale*

Proceed through step 1 of the Diamond Base, page 41.

1. Mountain-fold flaps A and B to the center line in back. Then fold the entire model in half.
2. Form in order the two reverse folds indicated on flap C. (The first reverse fold bisects angle CAJ.) Form flap A into a rabbit-ear; repeat behind.
3. Form in order the two reverse folds indicated on flap C. (The first reverse fold bisects angle CLK.) Fold A in half; repeat behind. Reverse-fold the tip of flap D into the model.
4. Slit the tail only as far as shown. Then form in the front half of the tail the creases shown, swinging it down inside the model; repeat behind. Shape the nose with a reverse fold.
5. The two halves of the tail must now be treated differently. C2, the back half, is pulled out of the model into the position shown in fig. 6. The front half, C1, is simply mountain-folded as indicated.
6. Insert the mountain-crease of C2 down into the pocket nearest you—no new creases are made. This locks the entire tail-assembly together.
7. The Whale rests naturally in a lifelike posture.

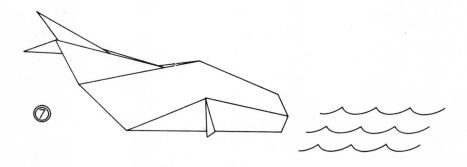

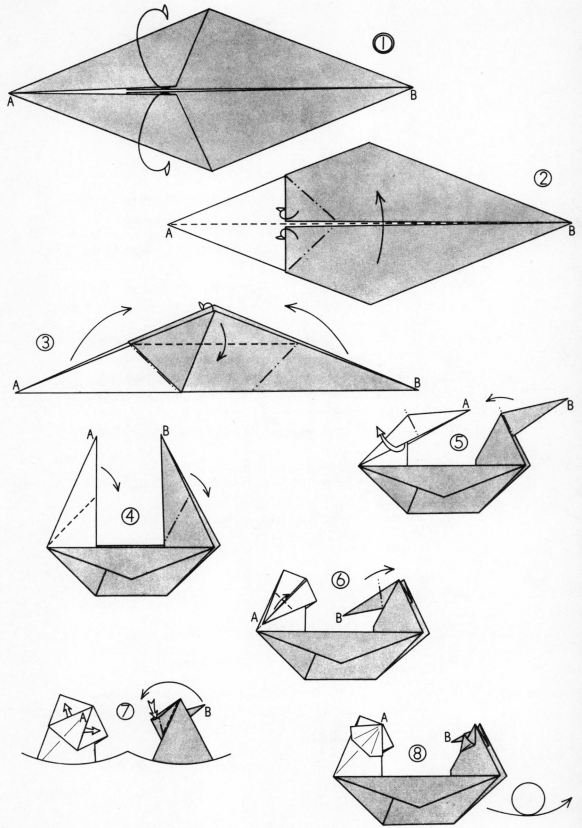

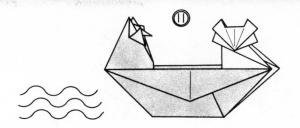

THE OWL AND THE PUSSYCAT *by Samuel Randlett*

1. Begin with the Diamond Base, page 41. Lift the near left flaps and fold them all the way around to the back of the model.
2. Mountain-fold the two loose corners inward. Fold the model in half.
3. Reverse-fold flap A upward along the folded edge. Reverse-fold flap B upward at the same angle. Fold the near top edge of the boat downward; repeat behind.
4. Reverse-fold flaps A and B to the right.
5. Lift the near right edge of flap A and flatten the flap downward into the position shown in fig. 6. Reverse-fold flap B to the left.
6. Fold the tip of flap A upward. Reverse-fold flap B to the right.
7. This is a close-up view of the two heads. The Pussycat is on the left, the Owl is on the right. Open out the inner layers of flap A and flatten the flap. Reverse-fold B to the left to form the Owl's beak. Flatten the eyes of the Owl in squash folds. The Owl is now complete.
8. Turn the model over.
9. This is a close-up view of the Pussycat's head (flap A). Fold the top of the flap downward, bringing the head over to the front.
10. Slit the Pussycat's ears, being careful to cut only the front and back surfaces of the paper. Then sink the top of the head down into the model. Fold the right edge of the body to the left and into the body. Flatten the model.
11. By holding the front edge of the boat and pulling the back edge to the rear, the Owl and the Pussycat can be made to bob about in their boat.

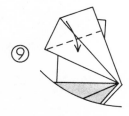
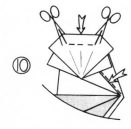

47

BOY ON A DOLPHIN by **NEAL ELIAS**, *page 76.*

PHEASANT by **ADOLFO CERCEDA**, *page 158.*

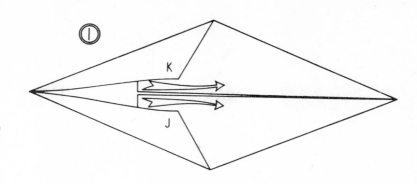

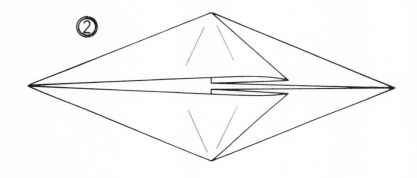

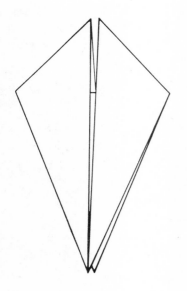

IV. FISH BASE

1. Begin with the Diamond Base, page 41. Reach in and grasp the two corners of the paper that are hidden under flaps J and K. Pull these corners out toward the right, and flatten them into the position shown in fig. 2.

2. The Fish Base is now complete. Its shape and "fins" suggest a fish, and several fish can be made from it. At the left the base is shown folded in half.

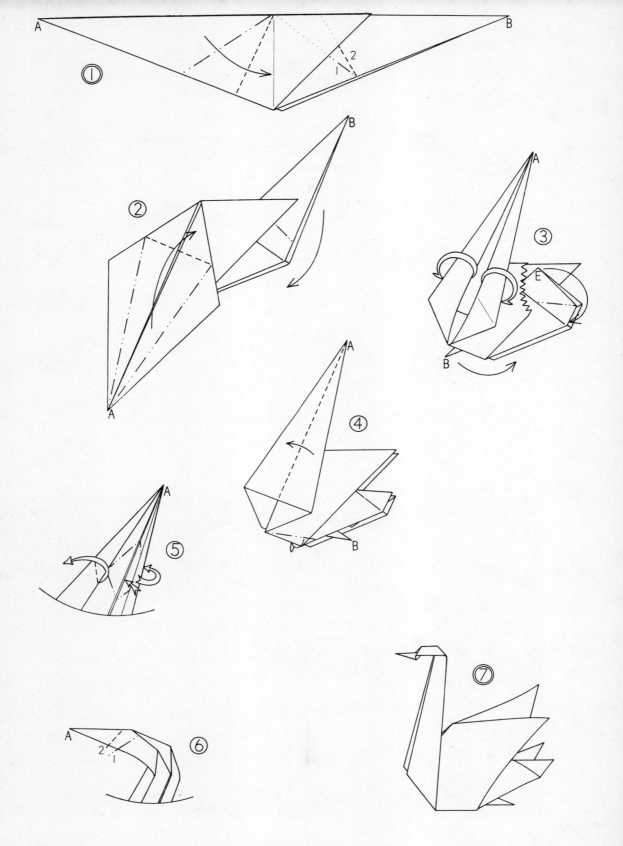

SWAN *by Ligia Montoya*

Begin with the Fish Base, page 49. Fold the base in half and rotate it to the position shown here.

1. Lift flap A and squash-fold it at the indicated angle. Form in order the two reverse folds shown on flap B.
2. Petal-fold flap A. Reverse-fold flap B downward.
3. Open out the front halves of flap A and wrap them around to the rear so that they lie on the back side of flap A. Reverse-fold flap E downward. Reverse-fold foot B to the right.
4. Fold neck A in half. Mountain-fold the bottom edge of the model up inside; repeat behind.
5. This is a close-up view of the tip of flap A, which will become the head. The near and far surfaces are swung down to the left in a sort of reverse fold, as indicated by the large arrows. At the same time the top of the head should be sunken in as shown by the small arrow.
6. Form the beak by making in order the two reverse folds shown on flap A.
7. The Swan makes an effective centerpiece when displayed on a mirror or polished metal tray.

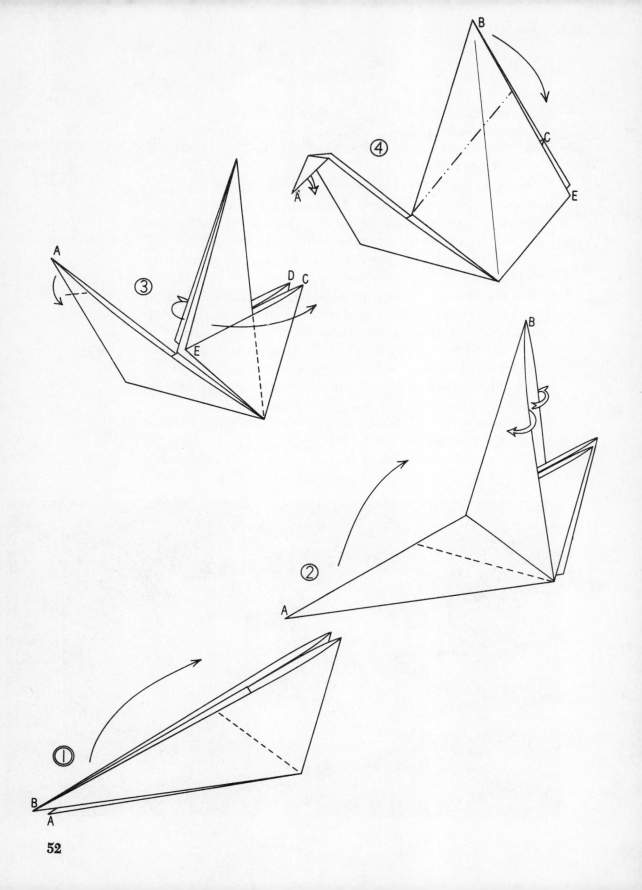

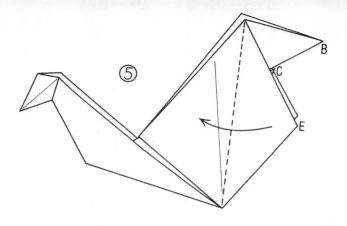

SQUIRREL   *by Fredric G. Rohm*

Use paper colored on both sides. Begin with the Fish Base as shown at the bottom of page 49. Fold it in half and rotate it to the position shown here.

1. Reverse-fold flap B upward; note that the reverse fold is made along an existing crease.
2. Reverse-fold A upward so that it lies along the lower left edge of flap B. Then reach into flap B and open out its inner layers, wrapping them around the outside of the flap.
3. Reverse-fold the tip of tail A downward. Book-fold flap E to the right; repeat behind.
4. Reach up into the tip of flap A and open its inner layers downward. Reverse-fold flap B down so that it lies along the upper edge of flap C.
5. Fold flap E to the left. Repeat behind.

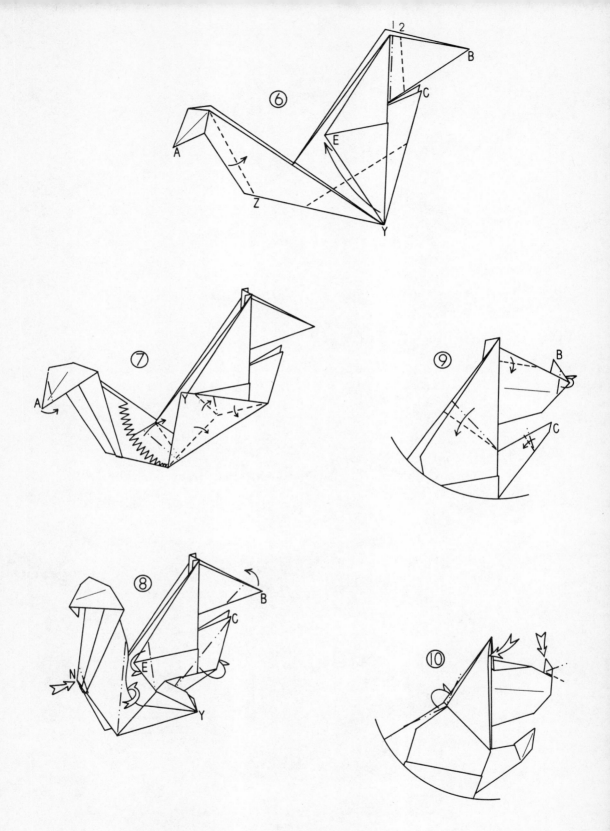

54

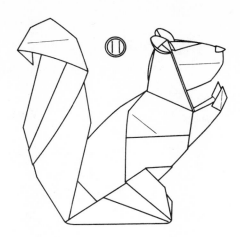

6. Fold the near left edge of tail A (a single layer) to the right. (The process continues into the model past point Z.) Repeat behind. Fold flap Y upward so that its tip lies just above point E. Repeat behind. Form in order the two reverse folds shown on flap B.

7. Reverse-fold the tip of tail A downward. Then make a pleat in the base of the tail by forming the mountain and valley folds shown; this adjusts the position of the tail so that it is more nearly vertical. (The front surface of the tail has been torn away for clarity.) Form flap Y into a leg by folding it into an off-center rabbit-ear; repeat behind.

8. Round off the left edge of the tail by sinking point N. Complete the tail by mountain-folding its right edge inward; repeat behind. Mountain-fold the tip of flap E inward; repeat behind. Make the foreleg by mountain-folding flap C in half; repeat behind. Reverse-fold nose B upward.

9. Crimp the neck to tilt the head slightly. Fold down the near top edge of the head—this automatically pulls the ear into shape. Repeat behind. Fold the right edge of nose B inward; repeat behind. Lift flap C and squash-fold it to form a paw; repeat behind.

10. Shape the neck with mountain folds; repeat behind. Open out the ears by squashing them downward and petal-folding them up. Squash the nose downward.

11. Compare the Squirrel with the Skunk that follows.

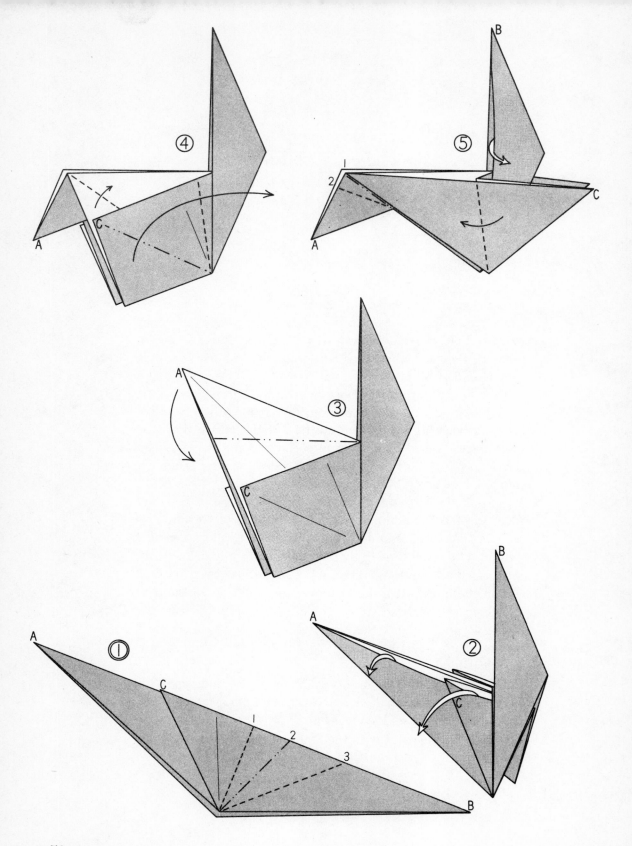

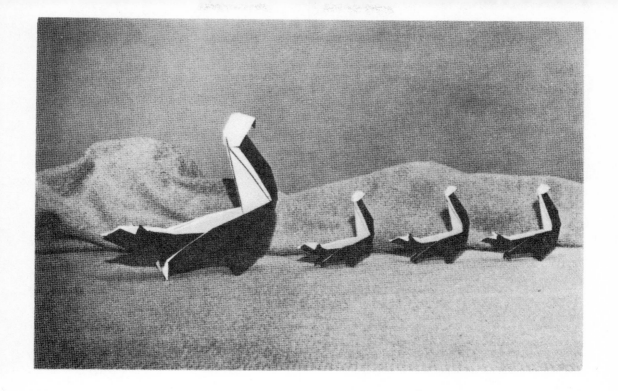

SKUNK *by Fredric G. Rohm*

Use paper white on one side. Begin with the Fish Base, page 49.
Fold it in half and rotate the base to the position shown here.

1. Make in order the three reverse folds shown on flap B. (The first fold is made by bringing B all the way over to A. The second fold runs along a crease line that already exists on the base. At the completion of the third fold, the right edges of the model should all be even.)
2. Open out flaps A and C as far downward as they will go. Flatten the model. Repeat behind.
3. Reverse-fold flap A downward so that its lower edge in fig. 4 is even with the top of flap C.
4. Lift flap C and pull it down to the right as far as possible; flatten the model. Repeat behind.
5. Make in order the two reverse folds shown on flap A. Fold flap C to the left as far as it will go; repeat behind. Open out the inner layer of tail B and wrap it around the outside of the tail to reveal the white side of the paper; repeat behind.

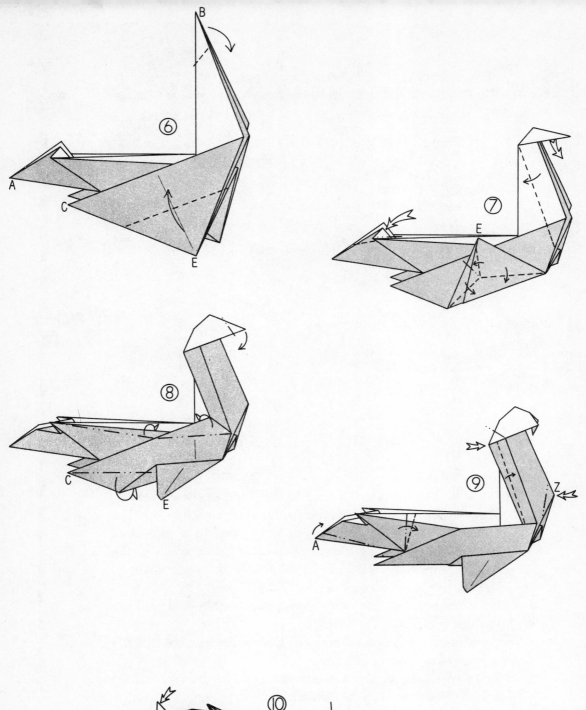

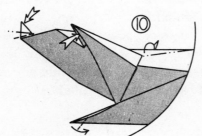

6. Fold E upward. Repeat behind. Reverse-fold the tip of tail B downward.

7. Open out the inner layer of the top of the tail, as indicated by the hollow arrow. (The same procedure is shown in detail in figs. 4 and 5 of the Squirrel, pages 52-53.) Then fold to the left the single layer nearest you. Form flap E into a leg by making it into an off-center rabbit-ear. Reverse-fold the ear downward. Repeat all of these operations behind.

8. Reverse-fold the tip of the tail. Mountain-fold C in half to form the foreleg; repeat behind. Mountain-fold the raw colored edge down into the model to enlarge the white stripe down the back; repeat behind.

9. Reverse-fold A upward. Crimp the neck slightly. Working from the bottom, fold the raw colored edge of the tail to the right, tucking it under at the top; repeat behind. Round off the tail by sinking point Z.

10. Squash-fold the nose. Open the ears by squashing them down, then petal-folding them upward. Shape the neck area by mountain-folding it inward as shown; repeat behind. Reverse-fold the forepaws.

11. The Skunk is related to Mr. Rohm's Squirrel, yet the two models are quite different in technique and appearance.

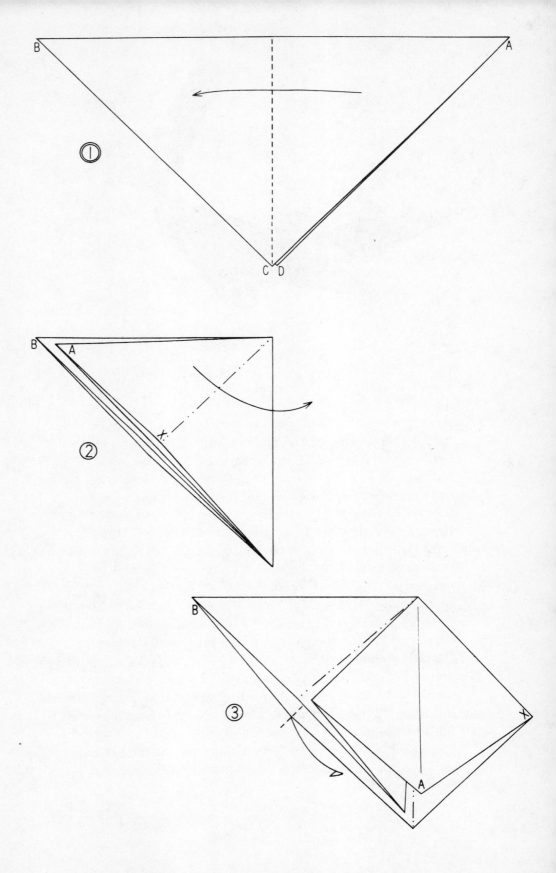

V. PRELIMINARY FOLD

Begin with a square of paper folded diagonally in half.

1. Fold the paper in half again, bringing the right side over to the left.
2. Lift flap A and squash-fold it. Watch the spot marked X.
3. Repeat step 2 behind.
4. The Preliminary Fold is the preliminary stage of many basic folds.

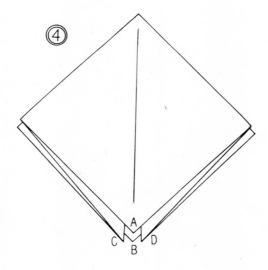

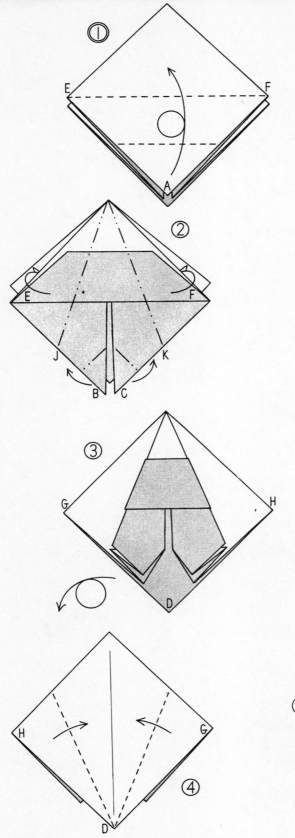

HOUSEFLY
by Ligia Montoya

Begin with the Preliminary Fold, page 60. The white side of the paper should be facing you.

1. Fold the tip of flap A up to line EF. Then fold up along EF.
2. Mountain-fold the upper edges of flaps E and F in to the center line. Reverse-fold flaps B and C so that their tips touch points J and K, respectively.
3. Turn the model over.
4. Fold DH and DG to the center line. As the model is flattened, a collar will form itself at the bottom (see fig. 5).
5. Square off the kite-shaped area into a rectangle. Pleat the tail. Turn the model over.
6. The Housefly is related to the traditional Japanese Cicada.

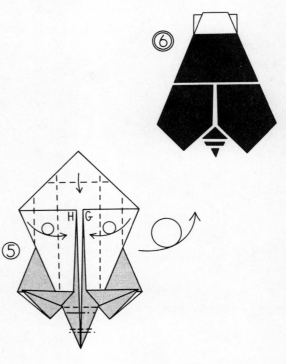

62

APE by LIGIA MONTOYA, *page 120.*

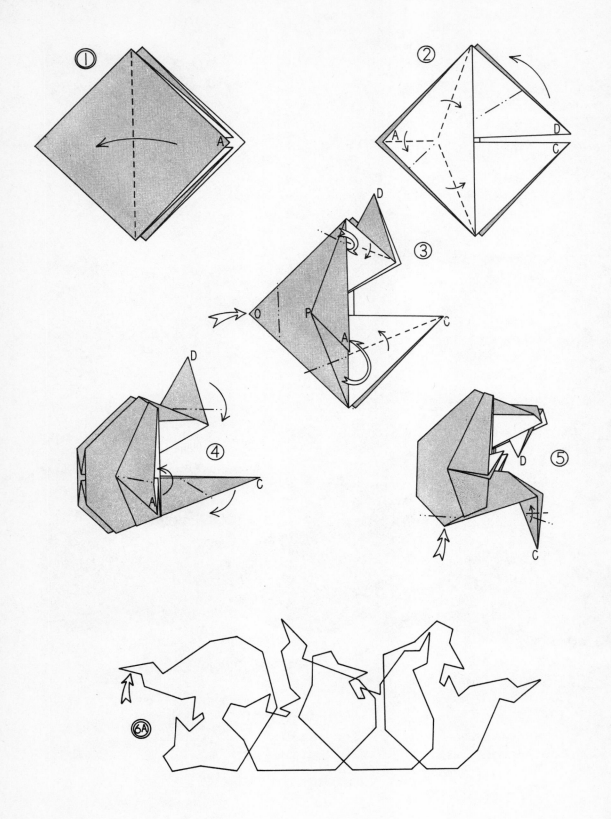

TUMBLING CHAN *by Harry Weiss*

Begin with the Preliminary Fold, page 60. Rotate it to the position shown here.

1. Fold flap A to the left. Repeat behind.
2. Form a rabbit-ear of flap A. Repeat behind. Reverse-fold flap D upward.
3. Sink point O so that its tip reaches point P inside the model. Working from the right, fold in half the near surface of flap C, tucking the lower corner up into the model as indicated by the hollow arrow; repeat behind. Treat the model similarly at the top.
4. Reverse-fold flap D downward to form the nose. Reverse-fold flap C downward to form the leg. Reverse-fold flap A upward to form a hand; repeat behind.
5. Crimp foot C upward. Sink the point indicated by the hollow arrow; repeat behind.
6A. Place Tumbling Chan on his head and strike his toe as indicated by the hollow arrow. He will do a somersault, rolling into the position shown in fig. 6B.
6B. For the best rolling properties, make sure that the near and far surfaces of the model are well spread apart. Tumbling Chan will rest in any of the six positions shown here.

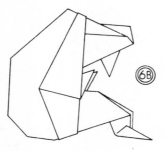 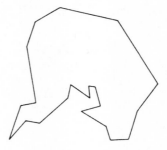

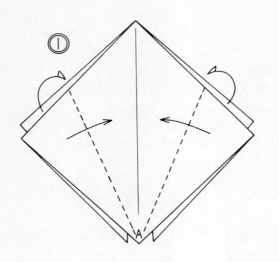

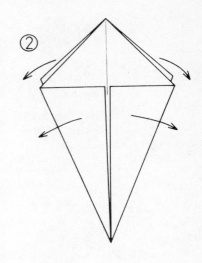

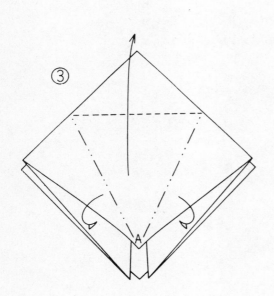

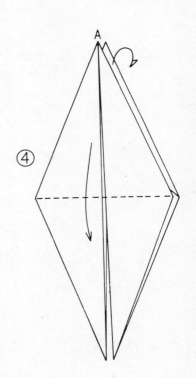

66

VI. BIRD BASE

1. Begin with the Preliminary Fold, page 60. Fold the lower right and left edges to the center line. Repeat behind.
2. Open out again.
3. Petal-fold A upward. Repeat behind.
4. Fold A down again. Repeat behind to complete the Bird Base, named for the classical Japanese Flapping Bird.

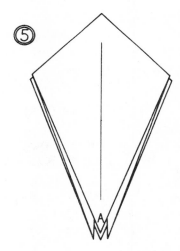

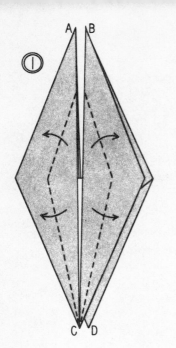

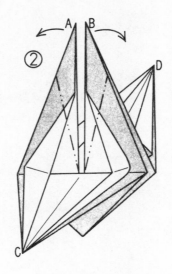

KISSING PENGUINS *by E. D. Sullivan*

Begin with the Bird Base as shown in fig. 4 on page 66. Turn the base upside down, bringing it to the position shown here.

1. Working from the bottom, fold the raw edges of flap C outward as indicated. (When this process is completed, flap C will point toward you.) Repeat behind.
2. Reverse-fold flaps A and B away from the center.
3. Reverse-fold the tips of flaps A and B toward the center to complete the heads.
4. Hold the back wing and pull the front one to make the Penguins kiss, or dance to music.

FARDEL BEARER by **GEORGE RHOADS,** *page 74.*

BUG by **GEORGE RHOADS,** *page 130.*

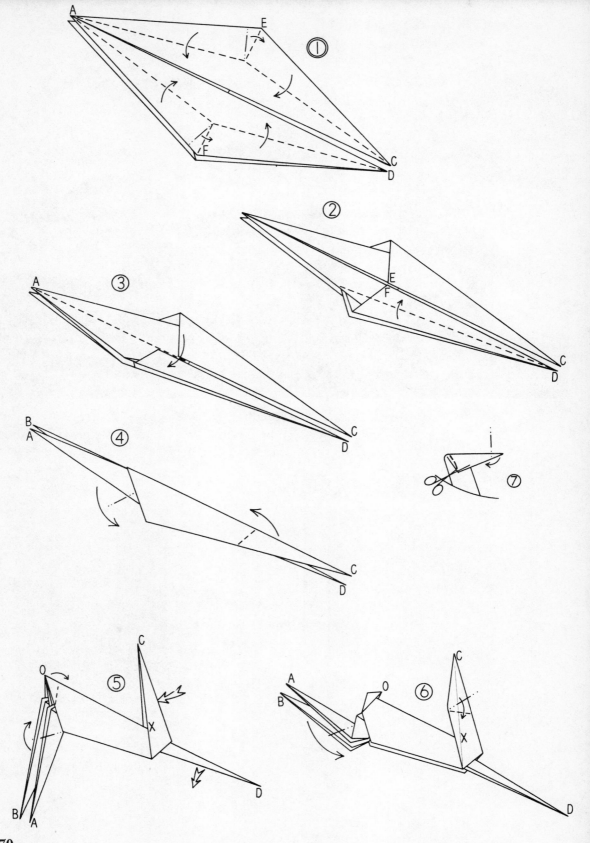

FAWN
by Harry Weiss

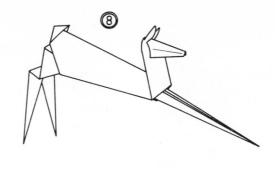

Begin with the Bird Base, fig. 4, page 66.

1. Fold the edges of flaps E and F to the center line and flatten the model (see fig. 2). Repeat behind.
2. (If your model does not look like this, pull the left edges of flaps E and F free of the central area of the model.) Fold the lower edge up to the center line. Repeat behind.
3. Fold the near side of the model in half. Repeat behind.
4. Reverse-fold flaps A and B downward. Reverse-fold flap C upward to begin formation of the neck.
5. Reverse-fold legs A and B to the left. Reverse-fold point O toward the neck. Adjust foreleg D downward and flatten the model. Insert your finger into neek C from the right, pushing the inside of the neck to the left; then flatten the neck into the position shown in fig. 6. Watch the spot marked X.
6. Reverse-fold legs A and B downward. Crimp head C downward.
7. This is a close-up view of the head. Snip the ears and lift them upward. Blunt the nose with a reverse fold.
8. The pose is a large part of the Fawn's effectiveness.

BUTTERFLY by JACK J. SKILLMAN, *page 142.*

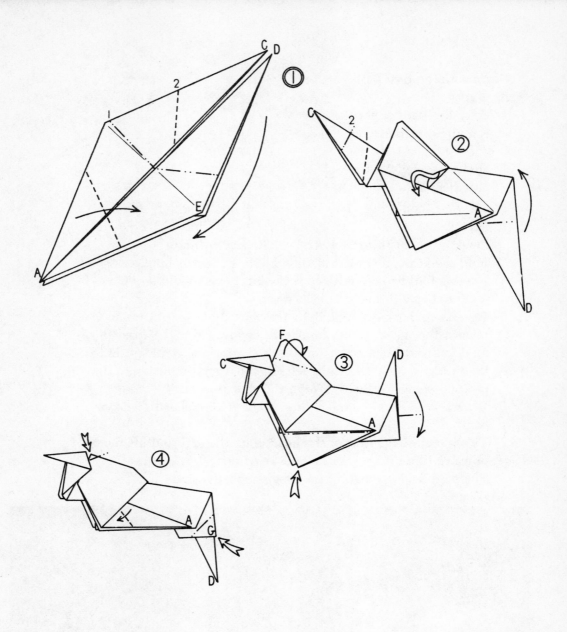

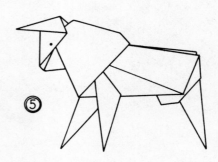

BULL *by George Rhoads*

Begin with the Bird Base as it is shown in fig. 4 on page 66. Rotate it to the position shown here.

1. Fold flap A so that its tip touches point E. Repeat behind. Make in order the two reverse folds indicated on flap C. Reverse-fold flap D downward.

2. Pull out the near left layer of the top of flap A and wrap it down around the outside of A. Repeat behind. Make in order the two reverse folds shown on flap C. Reverse-fold flap D upward.

3. Mountain-fold F down into the model. Repeat behind. Reverse-fold the bottom of flap A upward. Repeat behind. Reverse fold flap D downward.

4. Reverse-fold downward the point at the base of the horn. Fold foreleg A downward. Reverse-fold point G up into the model. Repeat all of these operations behind.

5. The Bull's forelegs should be set at different angles.

BULL by GEORGE RHOADS with **MATADOR** by **NEAL ELIAS,** *page 110.*

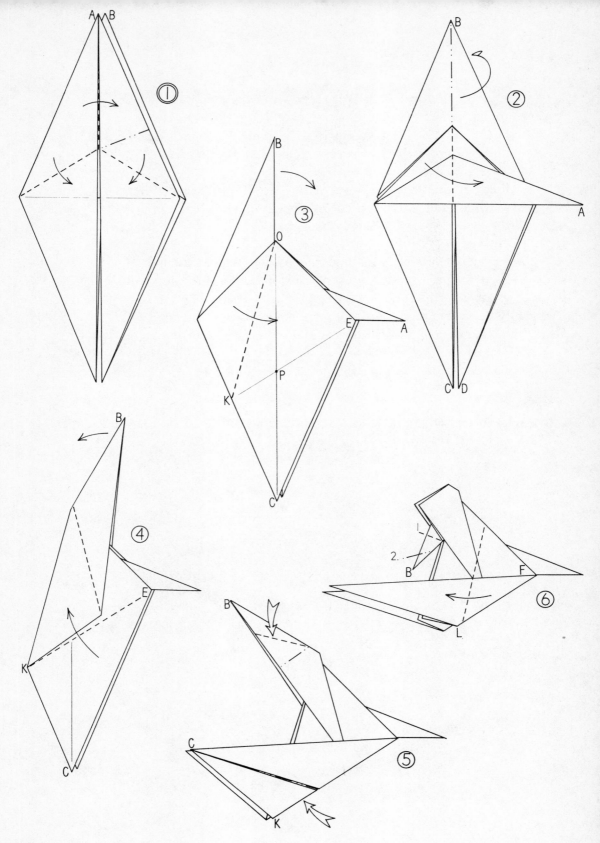

FARDEL BEARER *by George Rhoads*

1. Begin with the Bird Base as shown in fig. 4 on page 66. Form rabbit-ear of flap A.

2. Book-fold the front flap C and mountain-fold flap B so that the model looks like fig. 3 .

3. Locate point P, which lies midway between C and O. Form crease EPK to act as a guide. Reverse-fold flap B along line KO.

4. Reverse-fold flap B to the left. Fold flap C up along KE; repeat behind.

5. Crimp head B down between the sides of the hood. Reverse-fold K up into the model; repeat behind.

6. All edges should now be even on the bottom of the model. Make in order the two reverse folds shown on flap B. Fold flap F to the left; repeat behind. (The crease begins just to the right of point L. The upper edge of F must touch the intersection of hood and chin in fig. 7.)

7. Blunt the tip of the nose with a reverse fold. Make in order the two reverse folds indicated on flap C; repeat behind. (Note the position of the leg in fig. 8.) Grasp the model with your left hand beneath flap A to hold the paper in place as you pull A all the way to the right with your right hand.

8. Mountain-fold L down into the neck. Repeat behind. Narrow each leg in the same way that you have just shaped the neck. Make in order the two reverse folds shown on flap A.

9. Adjust the angle of the feet so that the model will stand. See page 69 for a photograph of the Fardel Bearer.

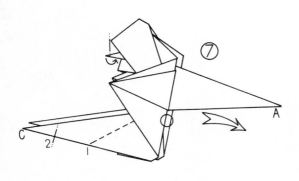

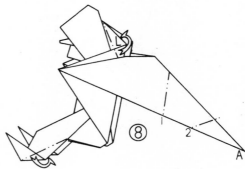

75

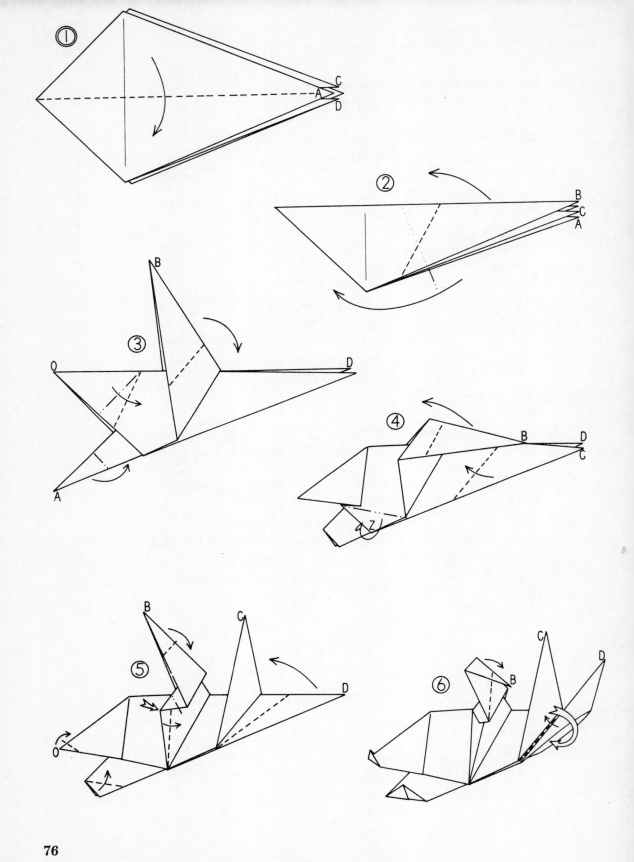

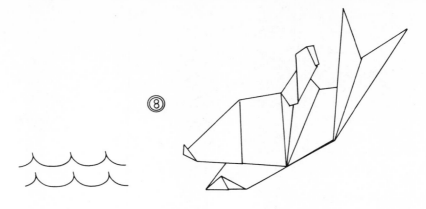

⑧

BOY ON A DOLPHIN *by Neal Elias*

1. Begin with the Bird Base, page 66. Fold the model in half.
2. Reverse-fold flap B upward. Reverse-fold flap A to the left.
3. Crimp flap O downward. Blunt the tip of flap A with a reverse fold. Reverse-fold flap B down to the right.
4. Reverse-fold flap B up and to the left. Mountain-fold corner Z up into the model; repeat behind. Begin formation of the tail by folding flap C upward.
5. Reverse-fold the tip of flap O upward. Fold the corner of the lower jaw upward; repeat behind. Reverse-fold flap B downward. Fold the left edge of the Boy to the right and flatten it; repeat behind. Reverse-fold flap D up so that it just touches flap C.
6. Reverse-fold the head of the Boy to the right; note the position of this fold. Begin to fold flap D to the left and to tuck flap C into the pocket in D.
7. Complete the tail by folding flap D all the way to the left, and tucking flap C as far as it will go into the pocket in D. Crimp the top of the Boy's head.
8. See page 48 for a photograph of the Boy on a Dolphin.

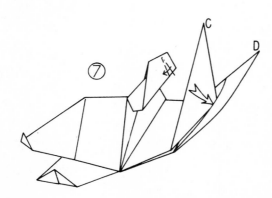

⑦

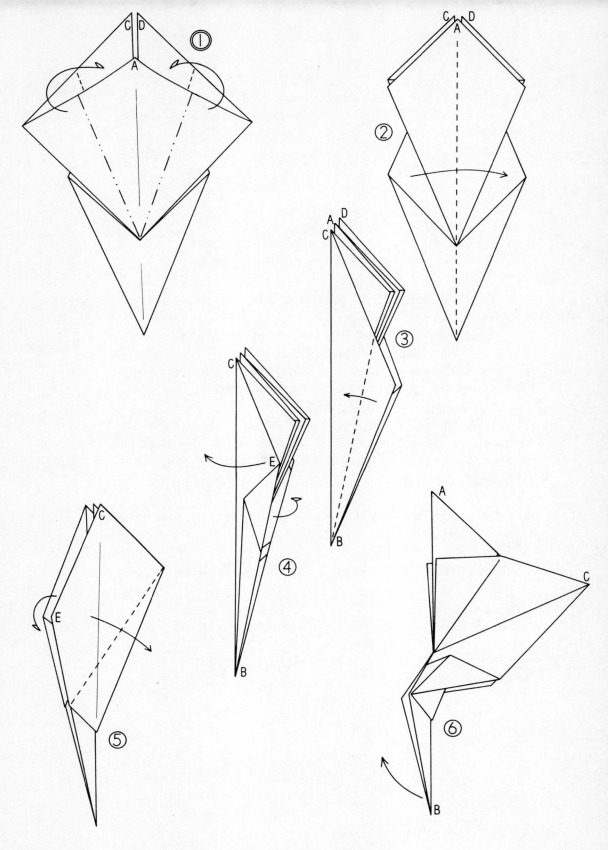

TURKEY *by Fredric G. Rohm*

Proceed through step 2 of the Bird Base, page 66. Then, leaving flap A as it is, petal-fold *only* the rear flap upward as in step 3 on page 66. Rotate the base to the position shown here.

1. Tuck in the lower edges of flap A so that they meet inside along the center line.
2. Fold the model in half.
3. Narrow flap B, leaving a small margin at the left. Repeat behind.
4. Book-fold flap BEC to the left. Repeat behind.
5. Fold flap C down toward the right. Repeat behind.
6. Grasp flap B by its tip and lift it up to the left as far as it will go. No new crease is made—flap B will change from a trough into a mountain as it is lifted.
7. Fold the upper edge of flap C downward and flatten the model. Watch the spot marked X. Repeat behind. Then open the small pocket downward as indicated by the hollow arrow, flattening in the Lovers' Knot move the solid point marked with a black dot. Watch this dot.
8. Reverse-fold neck B upward. Make in order the four reverse folds in flap A, which will become the tail. Working from the right, narrow flap C, tucking in L as indicated; repeat behind.

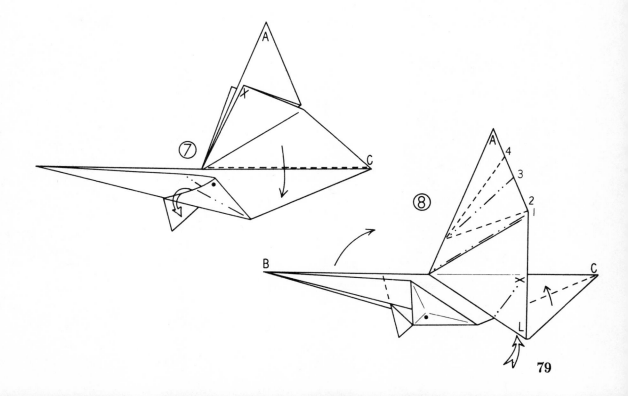

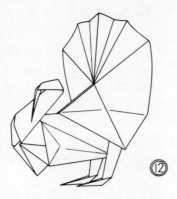

9. Make in order the two reverse folds shown on flap B. Reverse-fold the tip of tail A downward; then open the tail by folding its near surface to the left. Reverse-fold legs C and D downward.
10. Round off the top of the tail. Narrow the legs.
11. Reverse-fold the feet to the left. Then swing the right edge of the fanned tail to the rear, bringing the entire tail into the position shown in fig. 12.
12. The Turkey is made from a combination of Bird and Frog Bases.

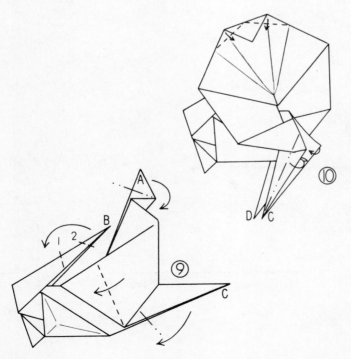

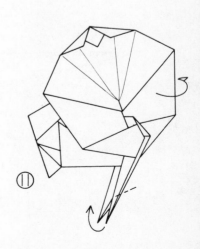

TURKEY by FREDRIC G. ROHM with HEN by ADOLFO CERCEDA, *page 154.*

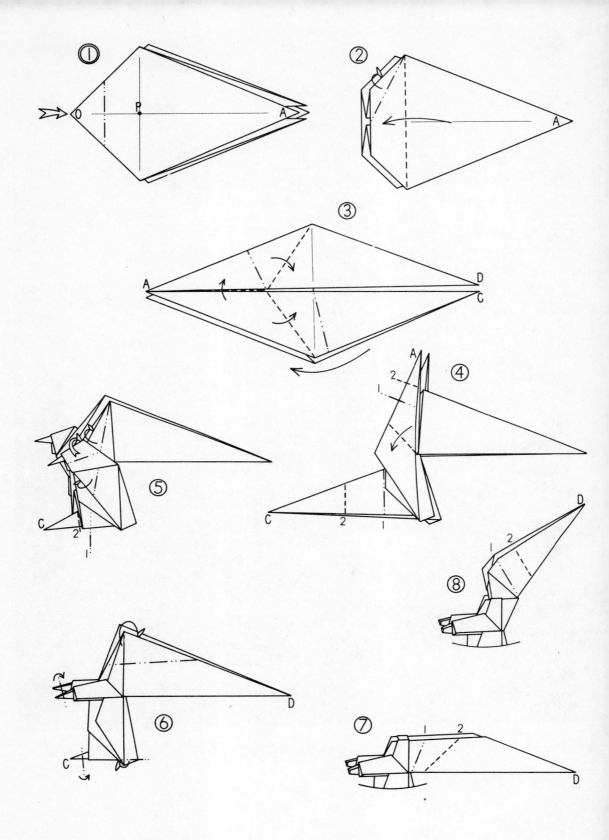

JOSEPH *by Robert Neale*

1. Begin with the Bird Base, page 66. Sink point O so that its tip goes as far into the model as point P.
2. Mountain-fold the upper left edge into the model. Repeat behind. Fold flap A to the left; repeat behind.
3. Form a rabbit-ear of flap A. Repeat behind. Reverse-fold flap C to the left.
4. Make in order the two reverse folds shown on flap C. Make in order the two reverse folds shown on flap A. Then fold A to the left; repeat behind.
5. Make in order the two reverse folds shown on flap C. (Note that the first lies inside the model.) Working from the top, narrow the outer layer of the robe by mountain-folding it in half; mountain-fold the forearm in half at the same time. Repeat behind.
6. Blunt the foot and the hands with reverse folds. Square off the bottom edge of the robe; repeat behind. Then mountain-fold the top of flap D down into the model; repeat behind.
7. Make in order the two reverse folds shown on flap D.
8. Make in order the two reverse folds shown on flap D.
9. Reverse-fold flap D to the left.
10. Complete the face by making in order the two indicated reverse folds.
11. Joseph, Mary, and the Baby from the Holy Family shown on page 85.

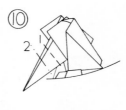

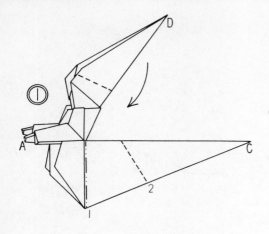

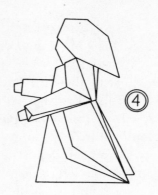

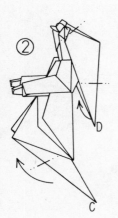

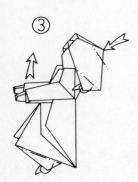

MARY *by Robert Neale*

Begin with the Bird Base and proceed through step 7 of Joseph, page 82. No folds, however, should be made in flap C.

1. Make in order the two reverse folds shown on flap C. Reverse-fold flap D downward.

2. Reverse-fold flap C to the left. Blunt the tip of flap D with a reverse fold. Shape the forehead with a mountain fold; repeat behind.

3. Square off the bottom of the robe. Adjust one of the arms upward. Shape the bottom of the hood with a mountain fold; repeat behind. Complete the hood by caving in its upper right corner.

4. See page 172 for the Baby.

HOLY FAMILY by ROBERT NEALE.

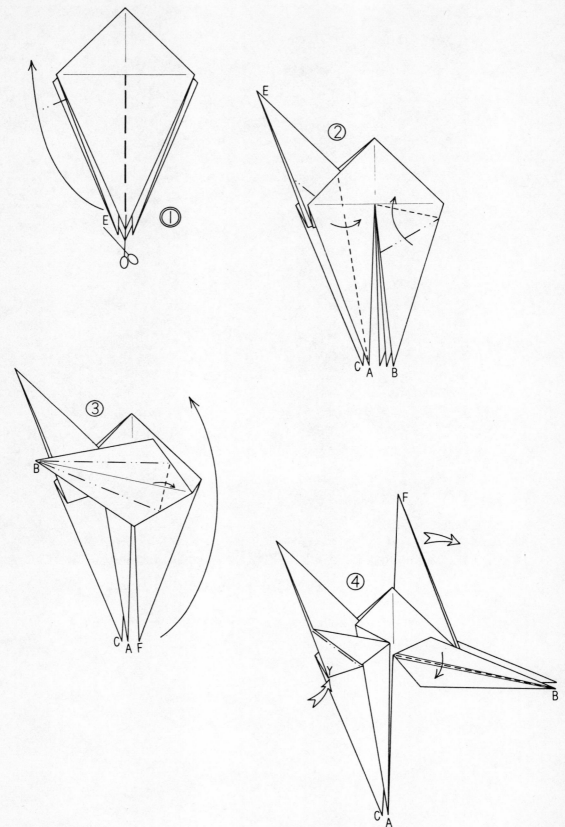

HALLOWEEN CAT *by Fredric G. Rohm*

1. Begin with the Bird Base, page 66. Slit the front and back flaps up to the crease line. Then reverse-fold flap E upward so that EA in fig. 2 is a straight line.
2. Fold flap A in half and flatten the area at the top into a collar. (The completion of this operation is seen most clearly in fig. 4.) Then lift flap B and squash-fold it at the angle shown. Repeat behind.
3. Petal-fold flap B to the right. Repeat behind. Reverse-fold flap F up as far as it will go.
4. Pull tail F to the right and flatten the model. Fold leg B in half; repeat behind. Reverse-fold corner Y upward.
5. Reverse-fold flap E to the right. Working from the top, fold the near surface of tail F in half and flatten the model; repeat behind. Reverse-fold leg B downward; repeat behind.
6. Fold the near left edge of the tail to the right. Repeat behind. Then turn the model over.

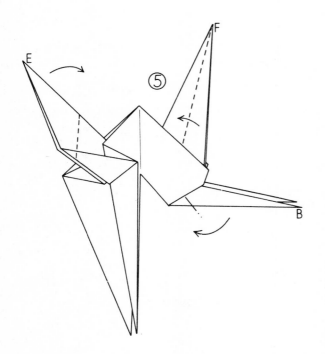

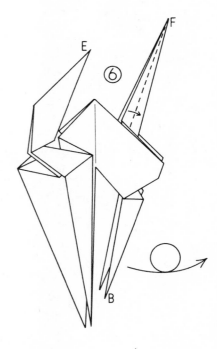

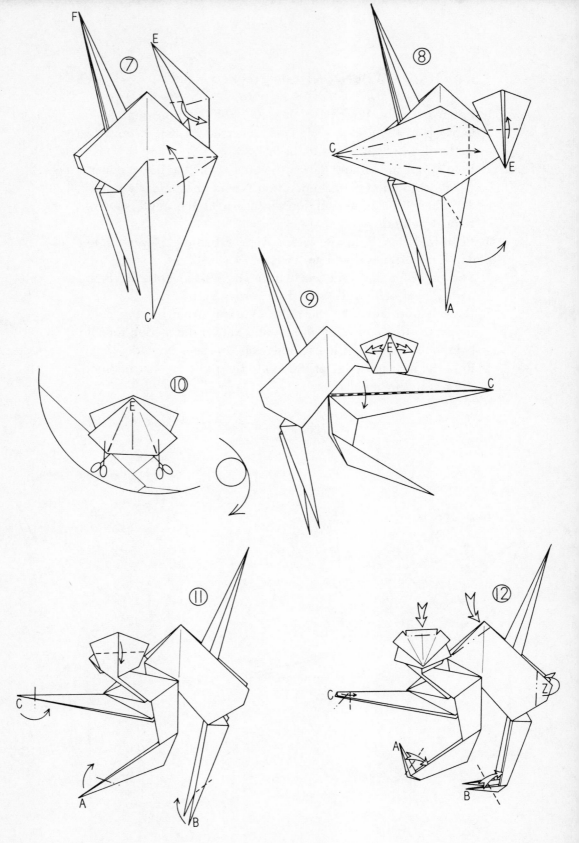

7. Lift flap C and squash-fold it to the left. Pull the near layer of flap E to the right, and flatten E down into the position shown in fig. 8.

8. Fold the tip of flap E up to the top. Petal-fold flap C to the right. Reverse-fold leg A to the right.

9. Open the inner layers of flap E out into the position shown in fig. 10. Fold leg C in half.

10. This is a close-up view of head E. Make the indicated slits, being careful to cut only the front and back surfaces. Turn the model over.

11. Blunt C with a reverse fold. Reverse-fold the tips of the other three legs to the left. Fold the head down.

12. Squash-fold the tip of C. Valley-fold the tips of A and B upward so that they are tucked into the grooves in the legs; repeat behind with the remaining leg. Sink the top of the head down. (The face is best locked in place when the edges of this sunken area touch the inside of the back layer of the head.) Mountain-fold corner Z inward; repeat behind. The Cat's back may optionally be shaped by sinking its point at the angle shown.

13. This model is among the most successful of all origami cats.

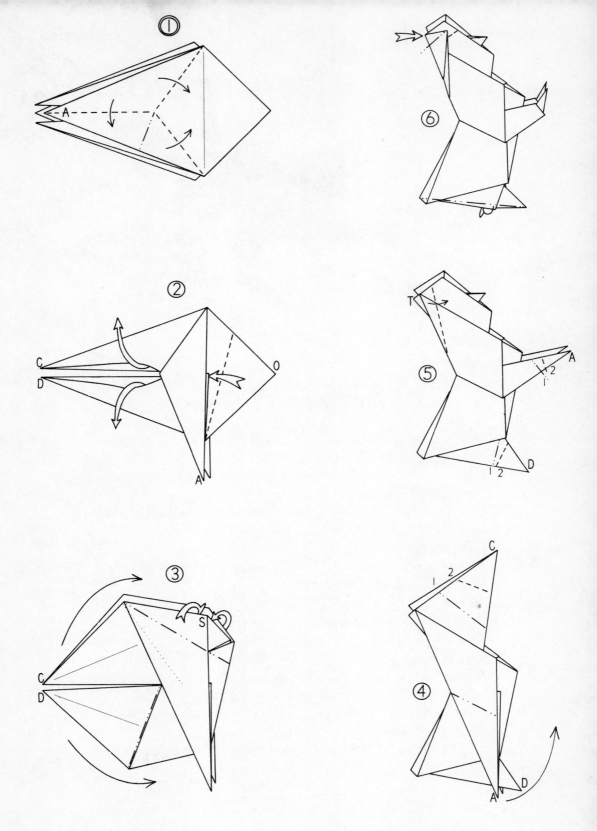

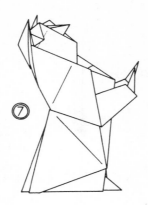

OPERA SINGER *by Neal Elias*

Begin with the Bird Base, page 66.
1. Form flap A into a rabbit-ear. Repeat behind.
2. Open the near layers of flaps C and D outward as far as they will go. Repeat behind. Tuck O into the pocket formed by flap A.
3. Fold area S down into the model in front and behind. Reverse-fold flaps C and D to the right. (Note that the reverse fold to be formed in flap C is indicated by an X-ray view.)
4. Reverse-fold arm A to the right. Repeat behind. Make in order the two reverse folds shown on flap C.
5. Fold corner T to the right. Repeat behind. Make in order the two reverse folds shown on flap A. Repeat behind. Make in order the two reverse folds shown on flap D.
6. Mountain-fold the bottom edge of the model inward. Form the horned helmet by reverse-folding the corner indicated by the hollow arrow. Repeat both operations behind.
7. The Opera Singer is seen here in the role of Brünnhilde.

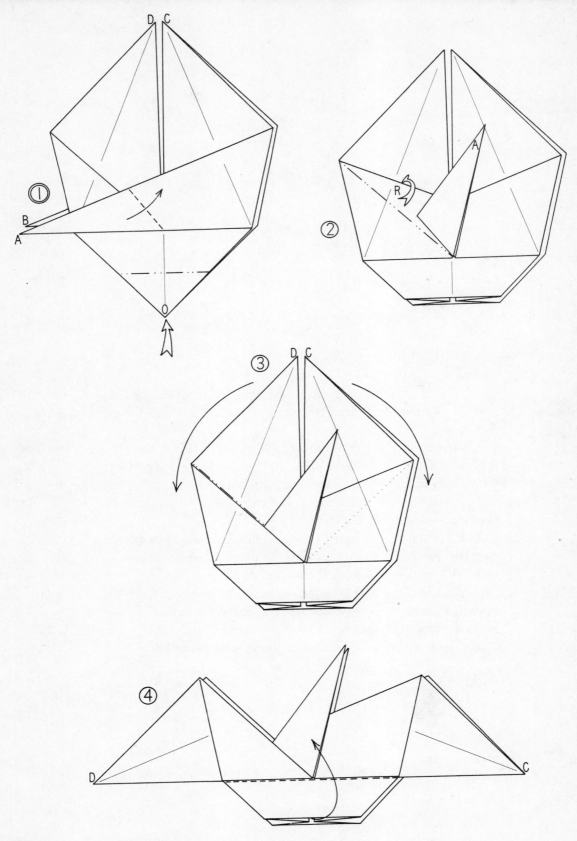

LION *by Neal Elias*

Use paper colored on both sides; ordinary brown wrapping paper is good. Begin with a large Bird Base and proceed through step 2 of the Opera Singer, page 90, leaving point O in place.

1. Sink point O up into the model so that its tip is even with the lower edge of flap A. Then fold flap A upward at the angle shown; repeat behind.
2. Mountain-fold area R (a single layer) down into the model. Repeat behind.
3. Reverse-fold flaps D and C outward.
4. Lift the nearest bottom edge of the model upward as far as it will go.
5. Book-fold the front of flaps C and D down as far as possible. Repeat behind.

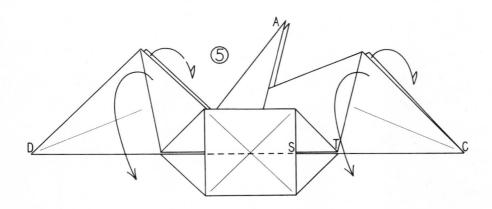

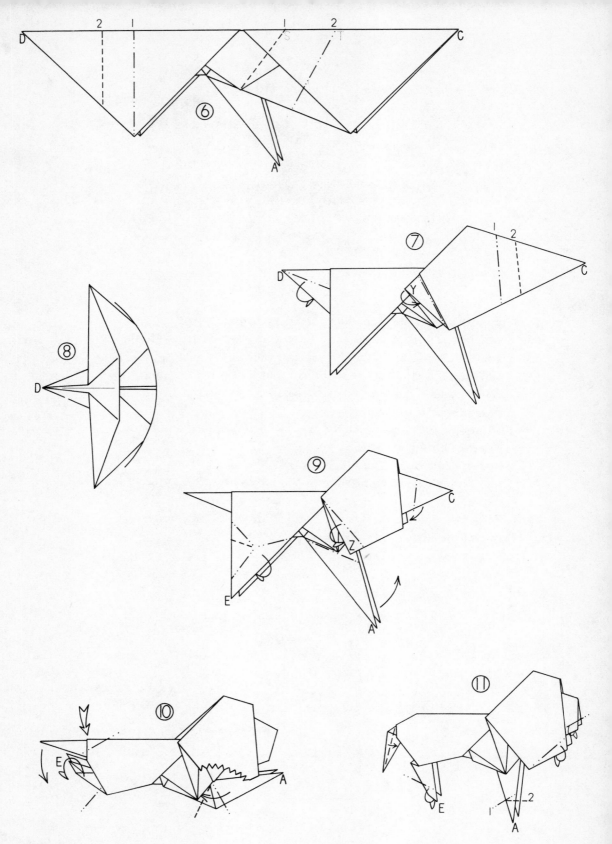

6. Make in order the reverse folds shown on flap D. Make in order the reverse folds shown on flap C. (The top of crease 1 in flap C lies at point S inside the model. The top of crease 2 lies at point T inside the model. See fig. 6.)

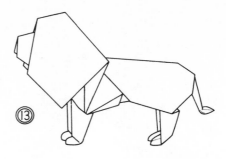

7. Working from its tip, narrow tail D by tucking its edges in; flatten the model (see fig. 8). Shape the mane by reverse-folding area Y to the right; repeat behind. Then make in order the two reverse folds shown on flap C.

8. This is a view of the tail from inside the model. Note the collar at the root of the tail.

9. Form flap E into a sort of off-center, mountain-fold rabbit-ear as shown. Repeat behind. Reverse-fold leg A upward. Repeat behind. Tuck area Z into the mane. Repeat behind. Reverse-fold flap C to the left.

10. Reverse-fold the tail (and a bit of the area just above it) downward. Mountain-fold leg E downward; repeat behind. Crimp leg A down; repeat behind.

11. Narrow the tail. Mountain-fold the tip of E to the right. Make in order the two reverse folds shown on leg A. Shape the mane and muzzle with mountain folds. Repeat all of these operations behind.

12. Open out the tip of the tail. Tuck in the area just above the foreleg; repeat behind. Blunt the forepaw with a reverse fold; repeat behind.

13. Neal Elias has used this original treatment of the Bird Base to produce several four-legged animals; see page 165 for a photograph of a Rabbit closely related to the Lion.

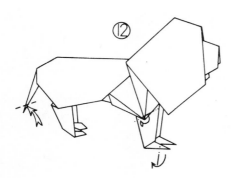

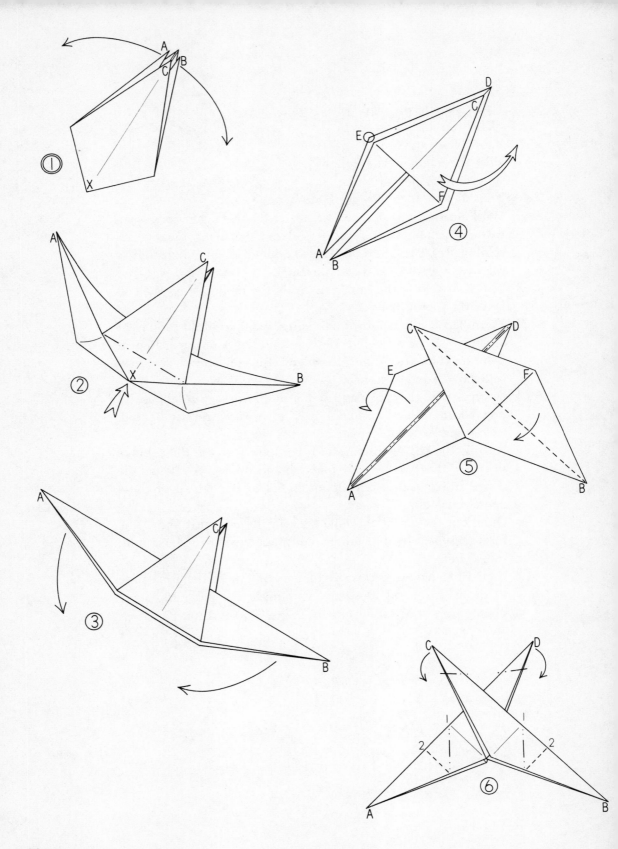

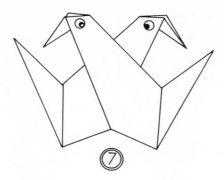

VII. BIRD BASE: STRETCHED FORM

TOGETHERNESS   *by E. D. Sullivan*

Begin with the Bird Base, page 66. Rotate the base to the position shown here.

1. Place your thumbs in the grooves at the sides of flaps A and B. Grasp these two flaps and pull them downward and out, until point X pops up into the center.
2. The action of step 1 is shown here in progress. Point X is about to disappear up into the groove that will run from A to B. Keep pulling the flaps. Then flatten the base into the position shown in fig. 3.
3. Reverse-fold flaps A and B downward as far as they will go.
4. Hold the rear left flap at point E. Grasp the near right flap at point F. Pull F up and to the right in a counterclockwise motion as far as it will go.
5. Mountain-fold along AD and valley-fold along BC.
6. Make in order the reverse folds shown on flaps A and B. Reverse-fold the tips of flaps C and D downward.
7. Add eyes to these suspicious lovebirds.

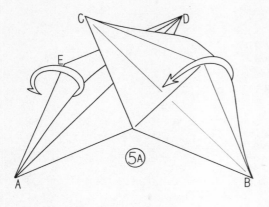

⑤A

APARTHEID
by Samuel Randlett

Begin with a Bird Base: the white side of the paper should be on the outside. Proceed through step 4 of Togetherness, page 96.

5A. Open out the near left layer of flap A and wrap it around to the rear. Open out the far right layer of flap B and wrap it around the front.

5B. Mountain-fold along AD. Valley-fold along BC. Proceed with step 6 of Togetherness.

7. The same device of wrapping a layer of paper to the rear can be used on the petals of the Purses to make each petal two-toned. Opposite petals of the first Purse may be so treated to indicate which should be pulled to open it.

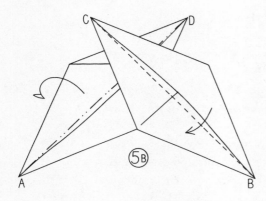

⑤B

⑦

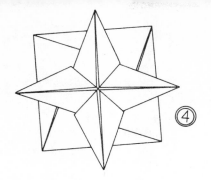

TWO PURSES
by Samuel Randlett

Begin with the Bird Base and proceed through step 2 of Togetherness, page 96.

1. Fold flap C down to the left as far as possible. Repeat behind, folding D in the opposite direction. Then lift the entire back half of the model into the position shown in fig. 2.

2. Mountain-fold flap A so that it matches flap B in fig. 3. (Note that the left edge of B falls halfway between points E and F.) Repeat with flap B.

3. Fold flap B toward the center of the model, tucking in its upper edges as indicated by the hollow arrow. Repeat with flap A to lock the Purse.

4. This Purse can be used to hold a gift such as a handkerchief.

A. The second Purse has the same structure as the first, but it is made from a pentagon.

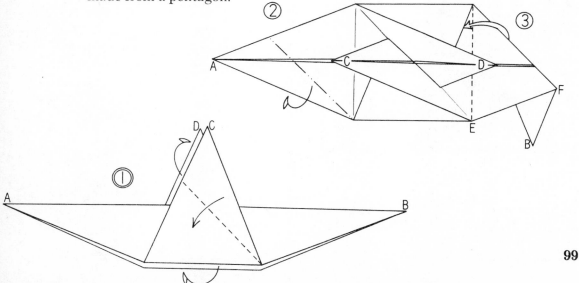

99

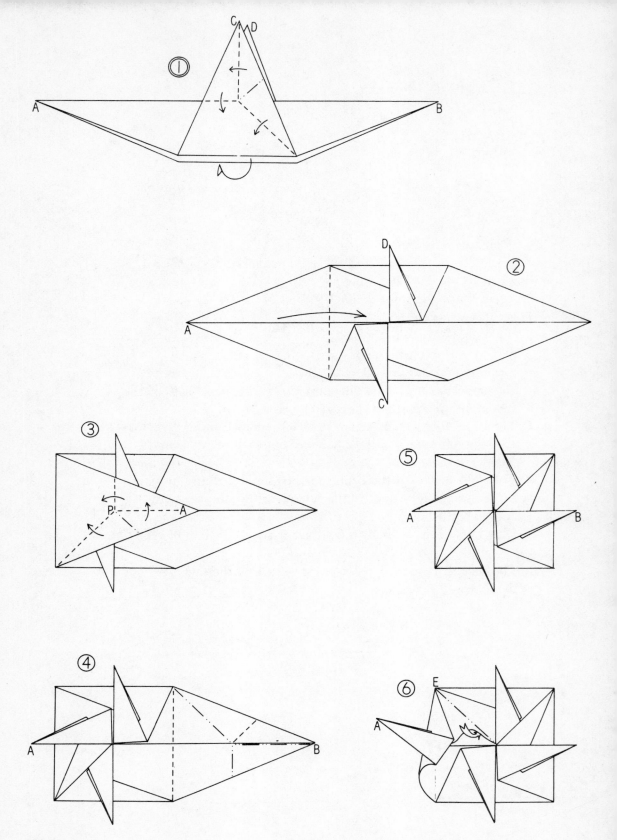

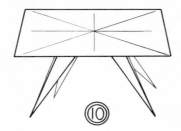

TABLE *by E. D. Sullivan*

Begin with the Bird Base, page 66, and proceed through step 2 of Togetherness, page 96. Use stiff paper.

1. Form flap C into a sort of rabbit-ear. Repeat behind.
2. Fold flap A to the right.
3. Fold flap A into a "rabbit-ear" analogous to C and D. (Note that point P lies over the exact center of the model.)
4. Repeat steps 2 and 3 with flap B.
5. Lift flap A and pull it slightly to the left.
6. Tuck the upper raw edge into the model as far as possible where indicated by the hollow arrow.
7. Tuck G into the pocket thus formed.
8. Repeat steps 7 and 8 with flap B.
9. Crease the legs and set the Table upright.
10. Each leg of the Table locks the next in place.

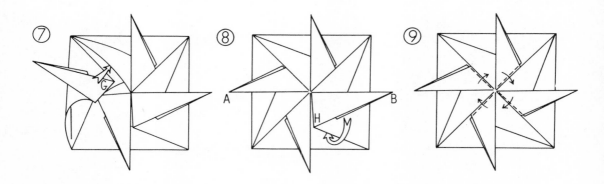

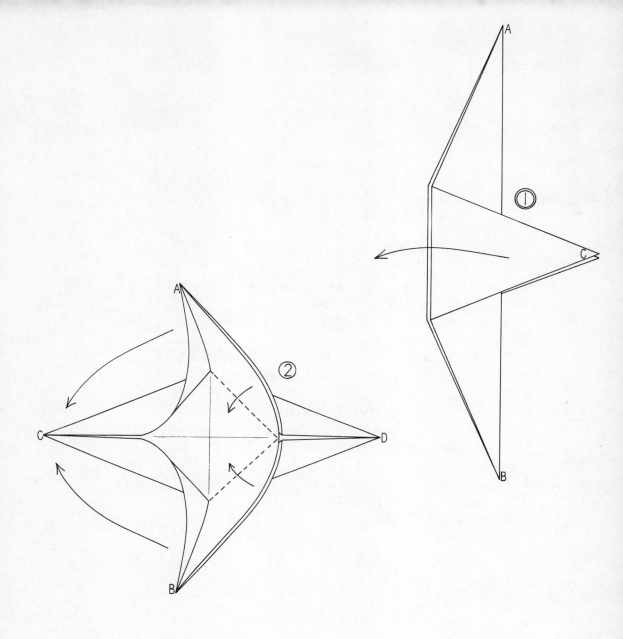

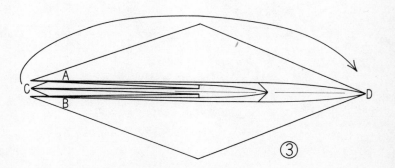

WHISTLER'S MOTHER *by Fredric G. Rohm*

Begin with the Bird Base, page 66. Proceed through step 2 of
Togetherness, page 96.
1. Pull flap C to the left.
2. Lay flaps A and B down on top of flap C.
3. Pull flap C behind the model all the way to the right, so that
   it touches flap D.
4. Valley-fold the model in half.

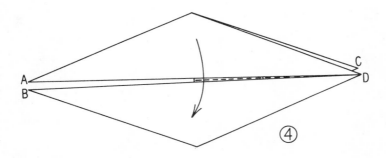

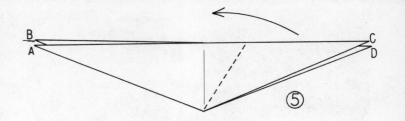

⑤

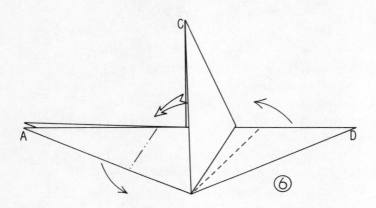

⑥

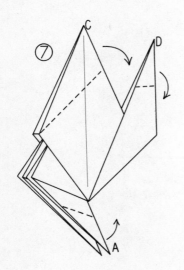

⑦

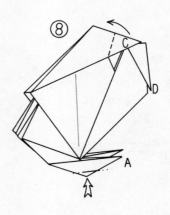

⑧

104

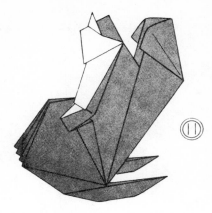

5. Reverse-fold flap C upward to the center line.
6. Reverse-fold flap A down and to the right; repeat behind. Open out the inner layer of flap C to the left; repeat behind. Reverse-fold flap D upward along the natural ridge inside the model.
7. Reverse-fold flap D downward. Reverse-fold flap C to the right. Reverse-fold flap A to the right; repeat behind.
8. Sink the bottom of flap A upward into the rocker; repeat behind. Reverse-fold flap C to the left.
9. Make the two crimps indicated; the larger one forms the arms, the smaller one forms the head. Open out the inner layer of flap D to the left; repeat behind.
10. Reverse-fold the tip of flap C to the right to complete the bonnet. Mountain-fold the left edge of the arm inward; repeat behind. Form the hand by a sort of crimp—note that the line indicated by the hollow arrow is a valley fold—and repeat behind. Then make the long valley fold shown at the bottom of the illustration.
11. Whistler's Mother will rock realistically when tapped with a fingertip.

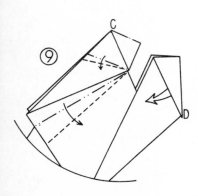

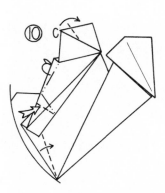

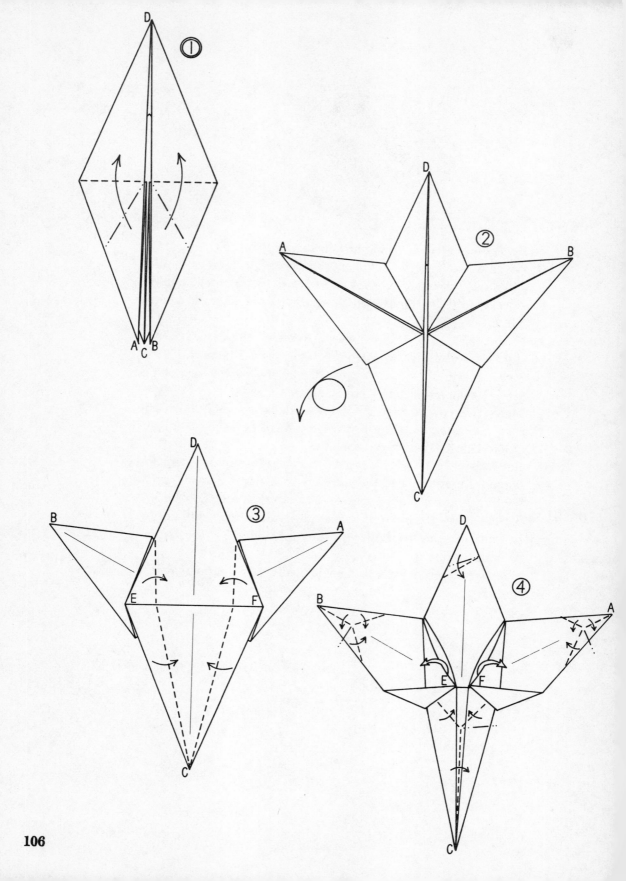

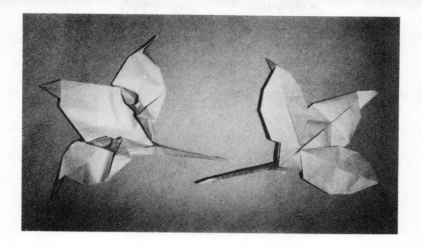

LEAF   *by Ligia Montoya*

Begin with the Bird Base, page 66. Proceed through step 2 of Whistler's Mother, page 102.

1. Lift flaps A and B and flatten each in an off-center squash fold.
2. Turn the model over.
3. Working from the bottom, fold edges CE and CF toward the center line (they should not touch it) and flatten the model.
4. Form flap C into a rabbit-ear. Form rabbit-ears of the tips of flaps B and A. Make a valley fold and then a mountain fold in the tip of flap D. Open out the pockets above E and F slightly, pulling points E and F upward a bit in the process. Do not flatten the model, but leave the pockets opened out in a three-dimensional way.
5. Fold down the upper edges of flaps B and A where they approach flap D. Narrow the stem. Turn the Leaf over.
6. Leaves are most effectively displayed in large numbers.

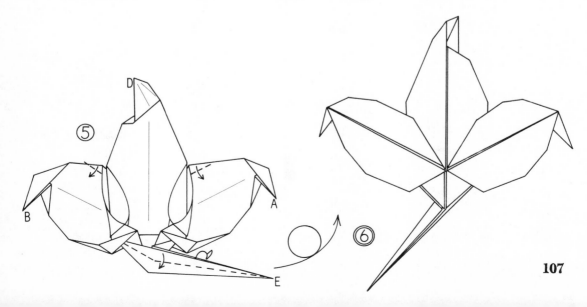

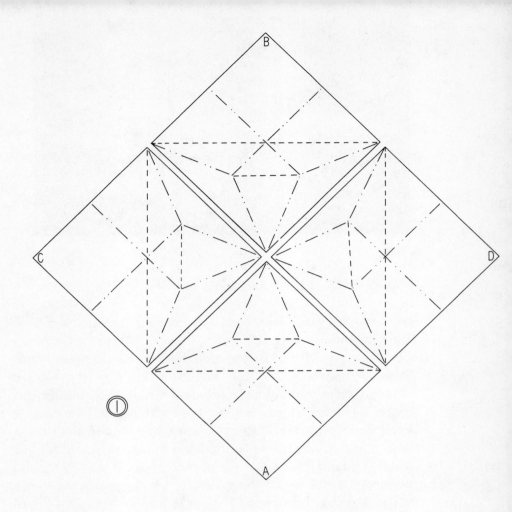

①

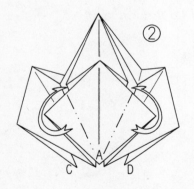

②

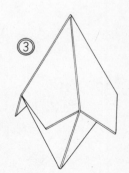

③

VIII. BIRD BASE: MULTIPLE FORMS

JAPANESE LANTERN   *by Jack J. Skillman*

1. Make four Bird Bases of equal size. Unfold them and lay them flat as shown here. Join their edges with cellophane tape in the back, to make one large square. Arrange the creases of the resulting square as indicated. (No new creases need to be made.) The center of the large square will rise toward you.
2. Mountain-fold the lower edges of the front of the model into the adjacent grooves. Repeat behind and on the sides, locking the model together. Turn the Lantern upside down.
3. The Japanese Lantern can be inflated or deflated through the hole at the top. It is properly folded from a single sheet. One way of doing this is to fold the corners of a square to the center, and make a Frog Base (page 140) from the resulting smaller square. When the base is opened out flat, its crease pattern will be that of fig. 1, though some of its valley folds will have to be converted to mountain folds.

The **JAPANESE LANTERN** by **JACK J. SKILLMAN** is shown here with **JOHN M. NORDQUIST**'s **ICICLES**, *page 118*, and **ORNAMENT**, *page 18*. Next to the **ORNAMENT** is a variation by Mr. Nordquist which begins with two squares.

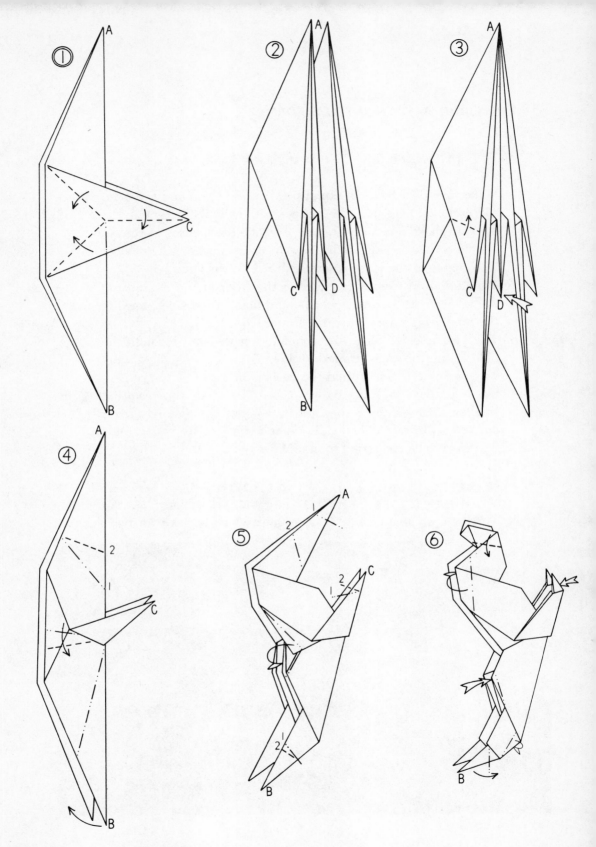

JOSÉ GRECO *by Neal Elias*

Begin with the Bird Base and proceed through step 2 of Togetherness, page 96.

1. Form flap C into a rabbit-ear. Repeat behind.
2. Make a duplicate base. Join the two bases together with cellophane tape along the single adjoining edge AD. This produces a stretched Double Bird Base. The base is properly made from a two-by-one rectangle.
3. Valley-fold flap C to the right. Repeat behind. Then reverse-fold flap D up to the left as far as possible, so that it points to tip A.
4. Begin formation of the legs by reverse-folding flap B to the left. Repeat behind. Crimp the entire body at the waistline. Make in order the two reverse folds shown on flap A.
5. Make in order the reverse folds shown on flaps B and C. Shape the back with mountain folds and flatten the model. Repeat these operations behind. Then make in order the reverse folds shown on flap A; note that both are of the same type.
6. Reverse-fold the foot to the right. Shape the thigh by sinking the left corner into the model. Mountain-fold the shin into the model. Shape the neck with a mountain fold. Fold down the near side of the head. Open out the hand slightly. Repeat all of these operations behind.
7. The hat should be crimped as shown. Adjust the angle of the feet so that the figure will stand. If José Greco is used as a matador, as in the photograph on page 73, a piece of red facial tissue makes an excellent cape.

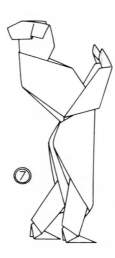

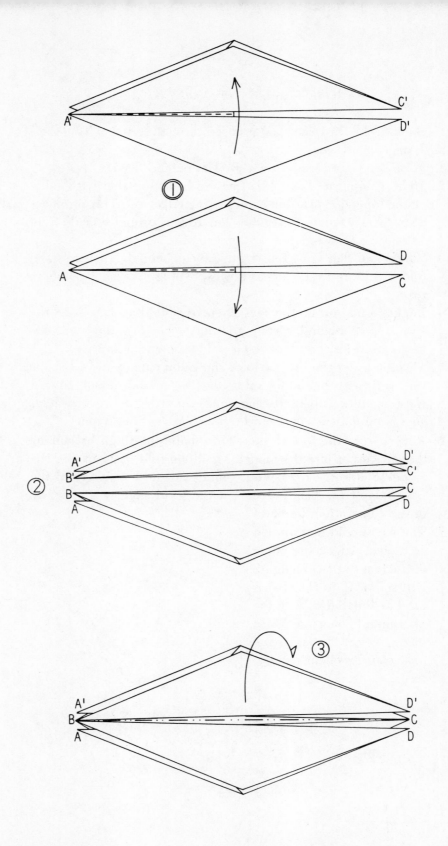

GIRAFFE *by George Rhoads*

Make two Bird Bases of equal size, proceeding with each through step 3 on page 66. Rotate the bases to the position shown here.

1. Fold both bases in half as shown.
2. Join the adjacent edges BC and B'C' with cellophane tape. Only the single back layer should be joined!
3. Mountain-fold the Double Bird Base in half. (The base is properly made from a two-by-one rectangle.)

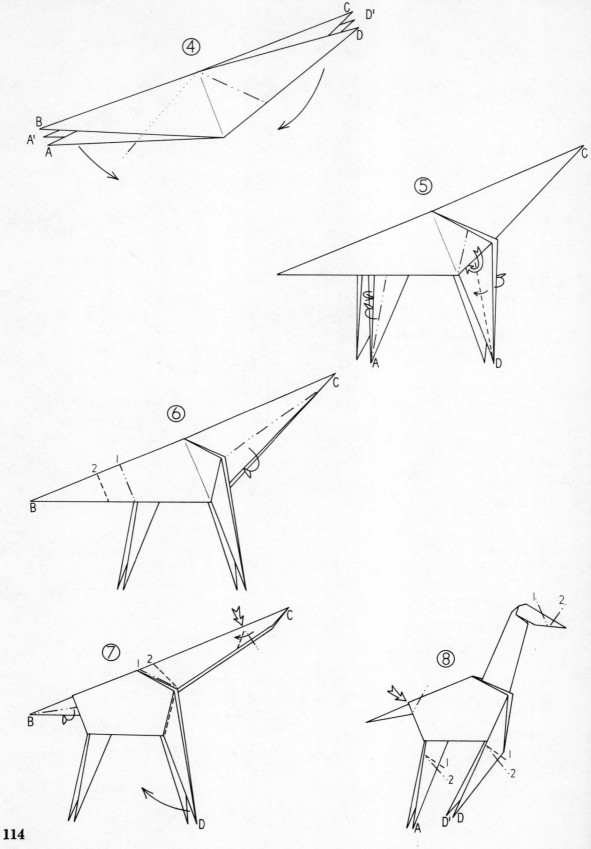

4. Reverse-fold legs A and D down. Repeat behind with A′ and D′.

5. Narrow foreleg D—tuck the upper edge into the shoulder. Repeat behind. Narrow hind leg A so that it equals the foreleg in width. Repeat behind.

6. Make the two reverse folds shown in flap B. Narrow neck C. (Note that the crease does not touch the tip of C.)

7. Narrow tail B. (See figs. 18 and 19 on page 138.) Reverse-fold the forelegs to the left. Make in order the two reverse folds shown at the base of neck C. Crimp the head down, caving in its top.

8. Reverse-fold the tail down. Make in order the reverse folds shown on the head, and on legs A, D, and D′.

9. Snip the outer layers of the head as indicated. Fold the outermost cut layer to the left. Repeat behind.

10. Blunt the tip of the inner flap. Then form it into a rabbit-ear. The completed horn is shown behind. Valley-fold the cut edges downward to suggest an eye. Repeat behind.

11. Two loose flaps will be found inside the chest. Fold one of these around the base of the neck. Then lock the body together by folding the other across the first and up between the neck-assembly and the inner surface of the body.

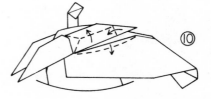

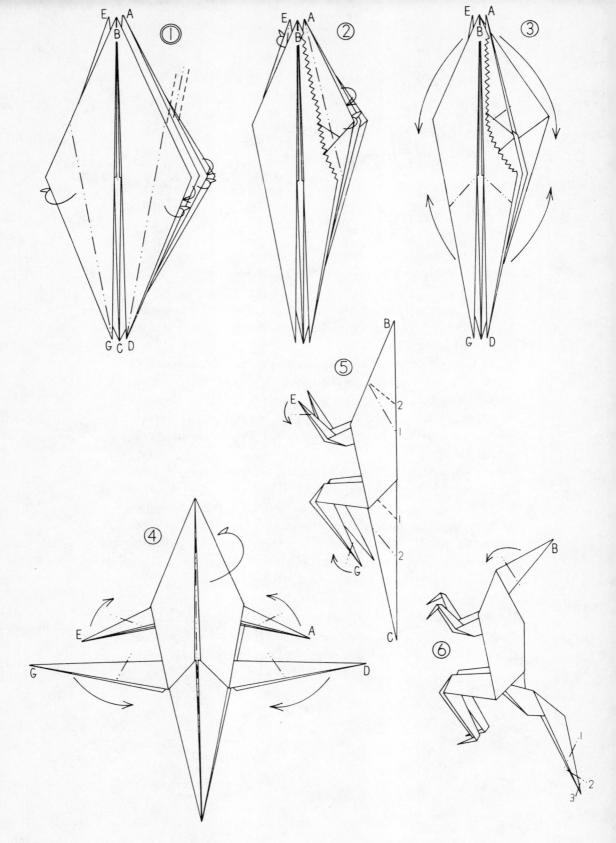

SPIDER MONKEY
by Neal Elias

Form a Double Bird Base by proceeding through step 2 of the Giraffe, page 112. Rotate the base to the position shown here.

1. Narrow the base by folding its lower edges inward to the center line. Note that the creases are alternately mountain and valley folds.

2. Narrow flaps E and A by folding their upper edges inward to the center line. (The front of flap B is torn away for clarity in this drawing and the next.)

3. Reverse-fold flaps E and A downward. Reverse-fold flaps G and D upward.

4. Reverse-fold flaps E and A upward. Reverse-fold flaps G and D downward. Mountain-fold the model in half.

5. Reverse-fold the tip of flap E downward; repeat behind. Reverse-fold the tip of flap G upward; repeat behind. Form in order the reverse folds indicated on flaps B and C.

6. Reverse-fold flap B to the left. Form in order the three reverse folds indicated on the tail.

7. This is a close-up view of the head, with the front surface torn away for clarity. Blunt the tip of flap B with a reverse fold; then complete the muzzle by forming a sort of crimp where it enters the head. Round off the top of the head.

8. The Spider Monkey will cling to the edge of a drinking glass. See page 40 for a photograph of the Spider Monkey.

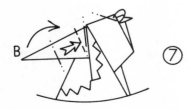

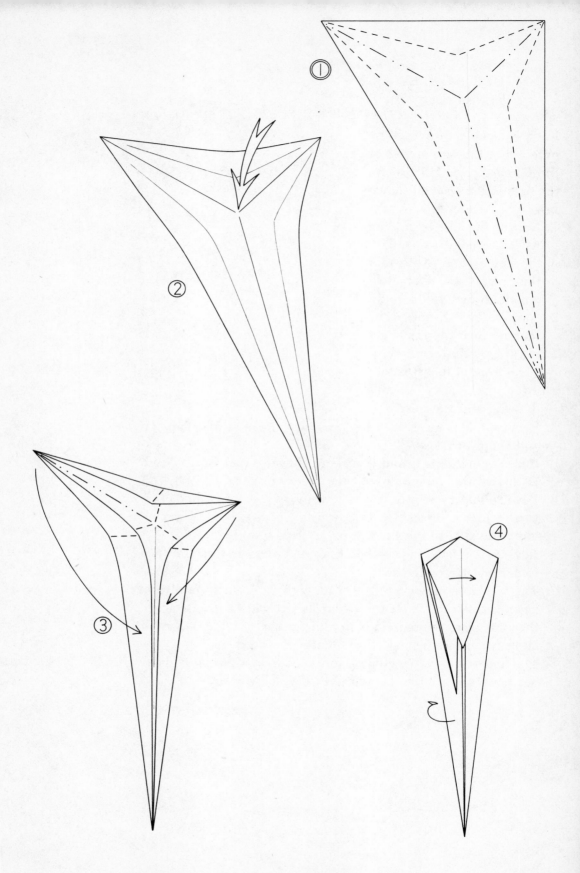

ICICLES
by John M. Nordquist

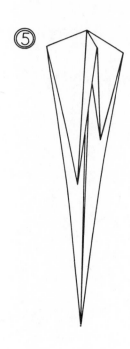

Begin with a 30–60-degree right triangle, made by cutting an equilateral triangle (page 33) in half, or with the aid of a draftsman's triangle.

1. Bisect each angle with a mountain fold. Then, working from the corners, fold the edges to the mountain creases.
2. Push back on the center point until it becomes concave.
3. Fold the shorter flaps downward so that their tips lie on the center line.
4. Arrange the Icicles into the three-dimensional form shown in fig. 5.
5. This simple model is an excellent Christmas decoration—see the photograph on page 109.

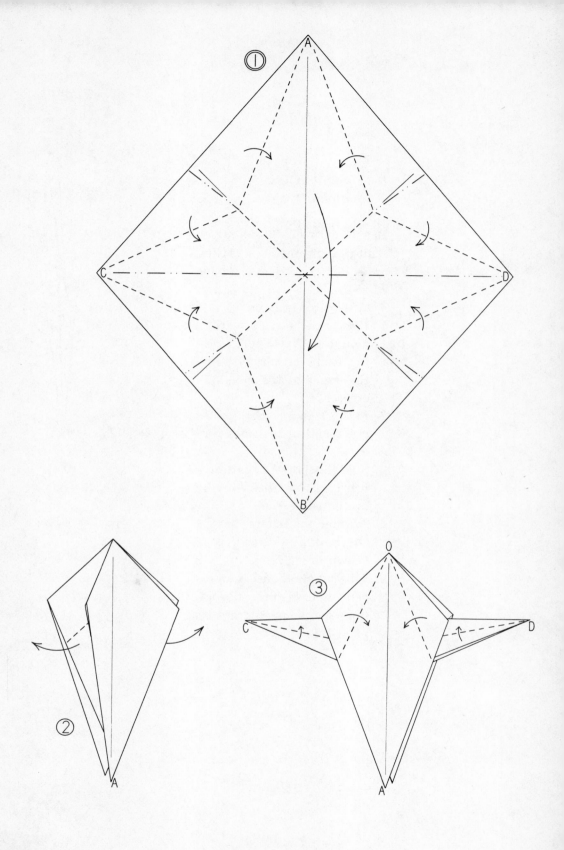

APE *by Ligia Montoya*

Begin with a five-by-six rectangle. Cut the corners off equally to make the diamond-shaped sheet shown here. The white side of the paper should be facing you.

1. Working from the tip, fold the edges of flap A to the center line. Repeat with flaps B, C, and D. Use the intersection points of these creases to guide you in completing the Bird Base.

2. Reverse-fold the short side-flaps upward to begin the arms.

3. Working from point O, fold the near upper edges to the center line; at the same time, narrow arms C and D by folding their near edges upward. Flatten the model. Repeat behind.

4. Fold point O down to point P. Form in order the reverse folds shown on the arms. Locate point S, which lies halfway between A and P. Then form flap A into a sort of mountain-folded rabbit-ear. Repeat behind with flap B.

5. Form in order the reverse folds shown on flaps A and B. Shape the top of the head by making the small reverse folds indicated by the hollow arrows. Form the face by making a mountain fold and then a valley fold. Open the hands out downward.

6. See page 63 for a photograph of the Ape.

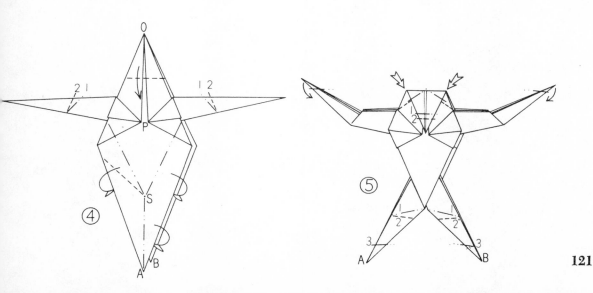

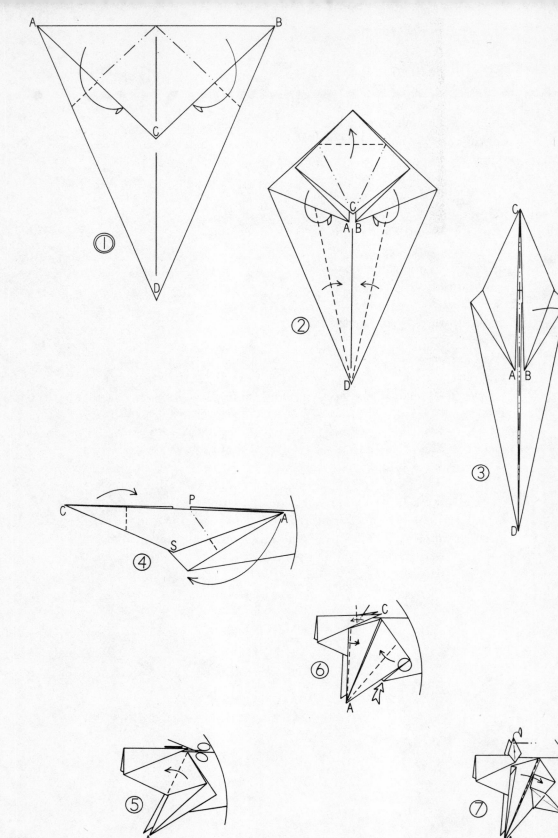

MOUSE *by Ligia Montoya*

Begin with a kite shape made by cutting along the dotted lines in fig. 1 of the Diamond Base, page 41. The white side of the paper should face you. Fold down the top as shown here.

1. Reverse-fold flaps A and B downward so that they touch the center line.
2. Petal-fold flap C upward. Working from the tip of flap D, fold its edges to the center line; continue the process out to the tips of A and B (see fig. 3).
3. Mountain-fold the entire model in half and rotate it to the position shown in fig. 4.
4. Reverse-fold flap C to the right so that it touches point P (the juncture of flaps C and A). Reverse-fold flap A downward; repeat behind.
5. Slit the ears. Book-fold the near surface of flap A to the left; repeat behind.
6. Lift and squash-fold each ear. Fold the right half of flap A to the center line; pinch its folded edge tightly as you do this, and the point indicated by the hollow arrow will begin to flatten itself in the Lovers' Knot move. Encourage this process, and enlarge the flattened area slightly; this serves to shape the underside of the Mouse. Then narrow the left margin of A to make the two halves of the flap equal in size. Repeat all of these operations behind with flap B.
7. Fold leg A in half; repeat behind. Round off the tops of the ears.

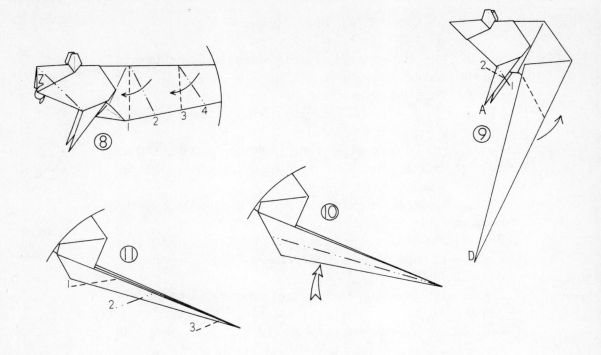

8. Mountain-fold area Z up into the model; repeat behind. Make two crimps in the body as shown. (Fold 1 lies a bit to the right of a crease line. Folds 1 and 3 are at right angles to the spine. Folds 2 and 4 are parallel to the shoulder.)

9. Reverse-fold tail D upward. Make in order the two reverse folds shown in leg A; repeat behind.

10. Narrow the tail by sinking its entire lower half upward.

11. Complete the tail by making in order the three reverse folds shown.

12. The Mouse's hind legs are so strongly suggested that their physical presence would be superfluous.

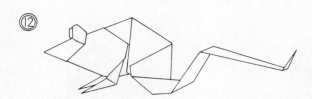

TYRANNOSAURUS REX, by GEORGE RHOADS, *page 128.*

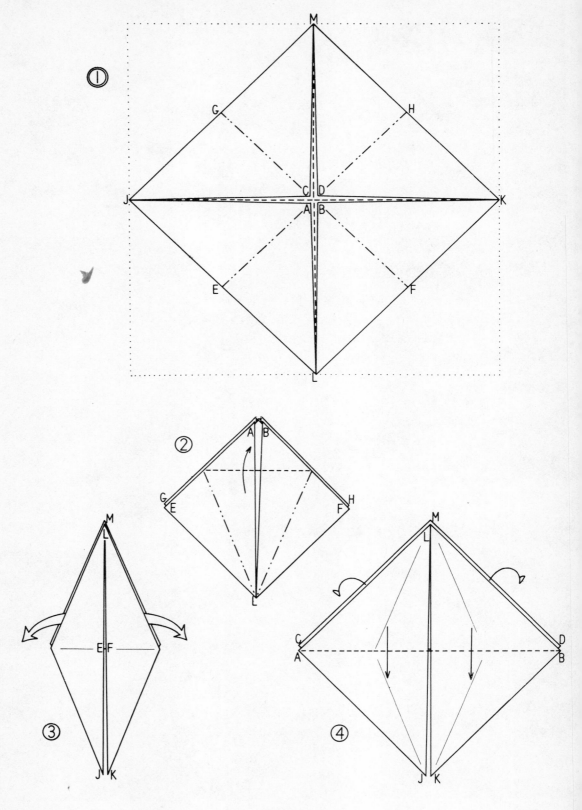

X. BLINTZ BIRD BASE

Begin with the large square ABCD shown in dotted lines in fig. 1; its colored side should be facing you. Fold the four corners A, B, C, and D to the center in blintz fashion.

1. Convert the square JLKM into a Preliminary Fold by making the creases shown. Ignore for the moment the fact that it is two layers thick. Points A, B, C, and D should be on the outside at the top of the completed Preliminary Fold.
2. Petal-fold flap L upward, exactly as in step 3 of the Bird Base, page 66. Repeat behind.
3. Now bring the single corners A and B outward, unfolding them from behind flap L. Repeat behind with C and D.
4. Fold point L down to the bottom. Repeat behind with M.
5. The Blintz Bird Base has eight points, twice the number of the simple Bird Base.

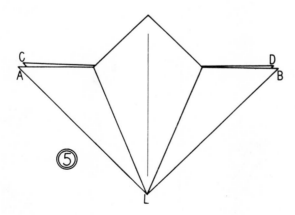

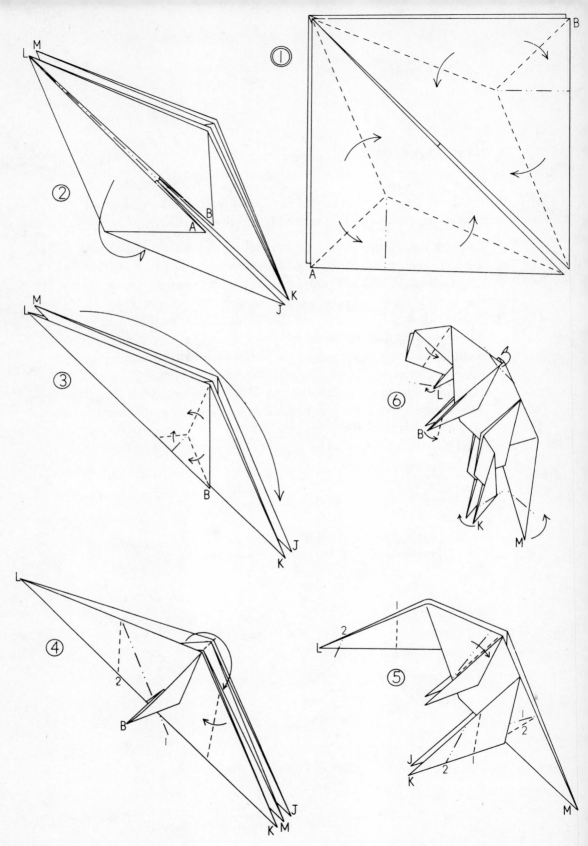

TYRANNOSAURUS REX   *by George Rhoads*

Begin with the Blintz Bird Base as it is shown in fig. 4 on page 126. Rotate it to the position shown here.

1. Form rabbit-ears of flaps A and B. Repeat behind.
2. Mountain-fold the model in half.
3. Form a rabbit-ear of flap B. Repeat behind. Fold flap M down so that its tip lies between points K and J.
4. Fold downward the short flap lying between the model's front and back halves, so that it points toward the tip of flap M. Make in order the two reverse folds shown on flap L. Fold flap K to the left; repeat behind.
5. Make in order the reverse folds shown on flaps L, K, and M. (Treat flap J like flap K.) Crimp the body down over the arms slightly.
6. Reverse-fold the tip of arm B downward. Reverse-fold the tip of leg K upward. Shape the back with a mountain fold. Repeat all of these operations behind. Then reverse-fold the tips of flaps L and M. Reverse-fold the head to the right—be careful not to tear the paper.
7. Round off the top of the head with a mountain fold. Repeat behind.
8. Eyes can be formed with a round or diamond-shaped ticket punch. George Rhoads makes a Gryphon from the Tyrannosaurus rex by pulling out the flaps that lie between the hind legs and the body, to form a pair of wings.

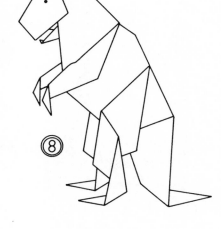

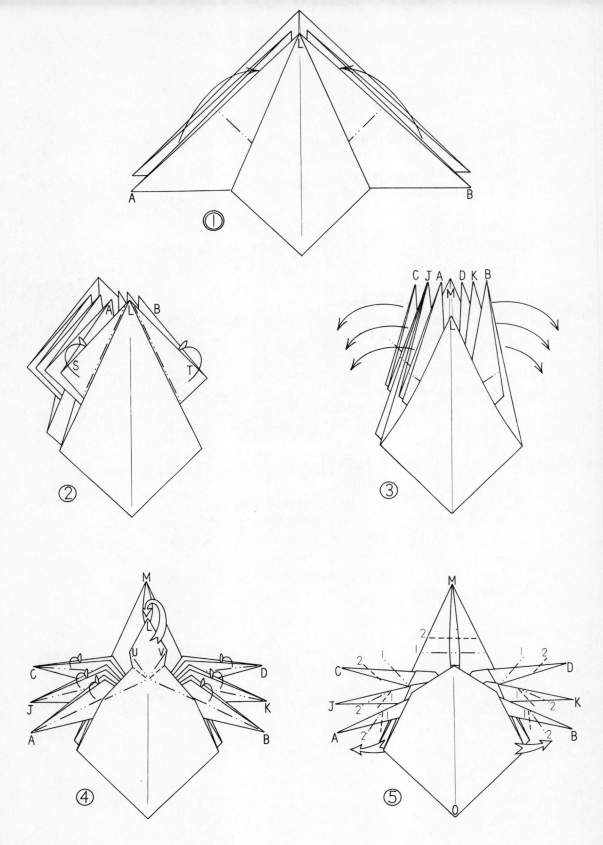

⑩

BUG   *by George Rhoads*

Begin with the Blintz Bird Base, page 126. Rotate the base to the position shown here.

1. Reverse-fold flaps A and B up to the top. Repeat behind.
2. Reverse-fold flaps S and T into the model. Repeat behind and on the sides.
3. Reverse-fold legs C, J, A, D, K, and B outward.
4. Narrow all six of the legs. Shape flap L into a hook by forming the mountain and valley folds shown. Then spread the central edges of flap M and insert this hook between them so that points U and V catch. Push the hook in and down to lock the body together.
5. Make in order the reverse folds shown in each leg. Form the mountain and valley folds shown in flap M. Grasp the far left and near right corners of the body and pull as indicated by the hollow arrows, so that point O will flatten itself somewhat as the body inflates.
6. Pull the central edges of head M out as far as they will go and flatten the head. Fold down corners Y and Z. Open out the inner edges of leg K; repeat with the left middle leg.
7. Form the tip of leg K into a rabbit-ear. Turn the model over.
8. Pull the inner edges of the head out as far as possible and flatten the top downward.
9. Complete the head by tucking in the tip indicated.
10. The Bug may be stuffed with cotton for display purposes.

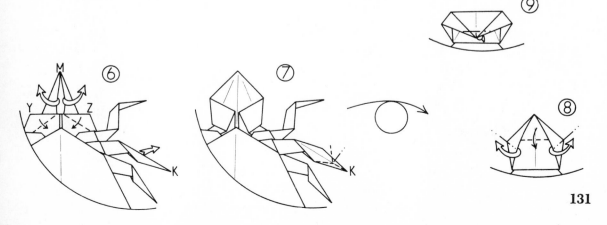

131

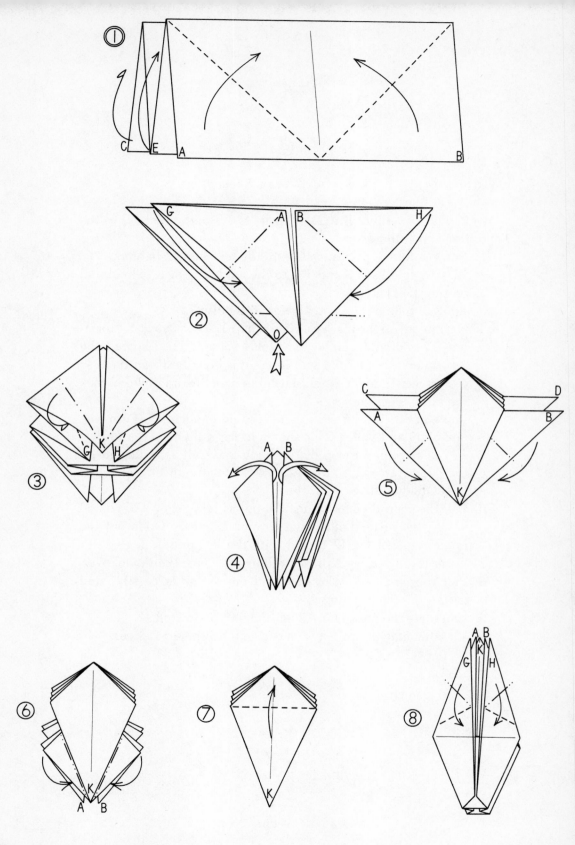

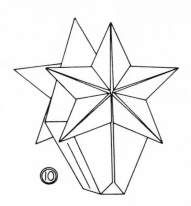

STAR FLOWERS   *by Fredric G. Rohm*

Begin with a two-by-one rectangle. Fold it into the configuration shown in fig. 1. Side AB is the width of the rectangle.

1. Fold flaps A and B up to the top of the model. Repeat behind. Then reverse-fold point E up at the same angle. Repeat on the right side of the model.
2. Sink point O up into the model. Reverse-fold flaps G and H down to the bottom; repeat behind.
3. Reverse-fold the lower edges into the model so that they lie along the center line. Repeat behind and on the sides.
4. Open layers A and B outward. Repeat behind with C and D.
5. Reverse-fold flaps A and B down to the bottom. Repeat behind.
6. Reverse-fold the lower edges into the model so that they lie along the center line. Repeat behind and on the sides.
7. Lift flaps K, A, B, G, and H up to the top. Repeat behind.
8. Lift flaps G and H and squash-fold them at the angle shown. Repeat behind.

9. Lift flaps A and B and squash-fold them at the angle shown. Repeat behind.
10. The pot containing the Star Flowers becomes three-dimensional when the back flower is held and the front one pulled forward.

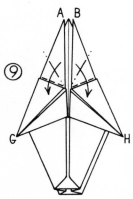

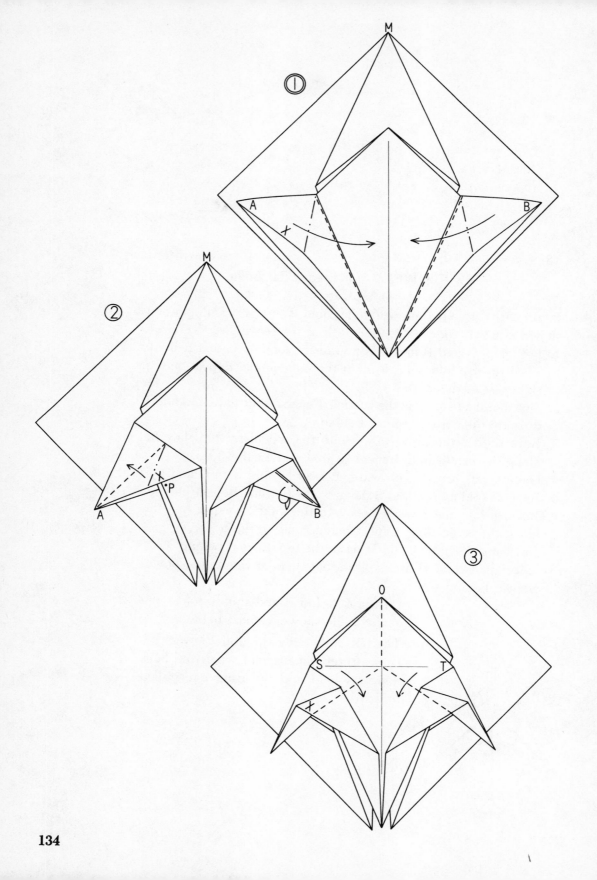

ELEPHANT *by George Rhoads*

Lift the rear flap of the Blintz Bird Base, page 126.

1. Crimp flaps A and B downward so that AM and BM in fig. 2 are straight lines. Watch the spot marked X.

2. Note the position of point P. Working from the tip of flap A, fold the raw edge of A up to its folded edge; then flatten the model so that the raw edge touches point P. Watch the spot marked X. (Flap B in fig. 2 shows this procedure completed.) Repeat the operation with the back of flap A. Repeat the entire step with flap B.

3. Lift flaps S and T toward yourself and fold them downward. (Point O will rise toward you.)

4. Squash-fold point O downward. Fig. 5 has been distorted to show clearly the completion of this squash fold.

5. Fold the model in half and rotate it to the position shown in fig. 6.

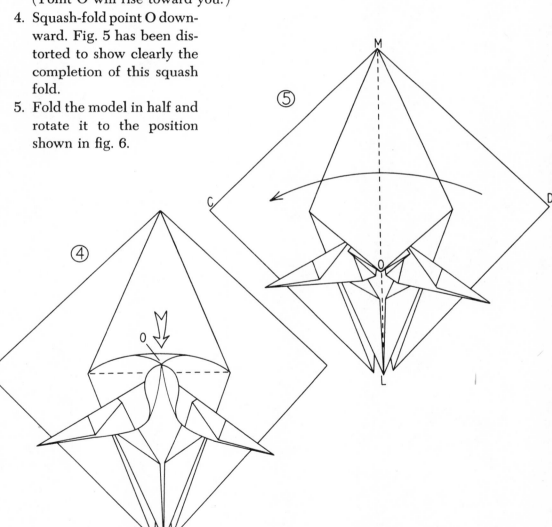

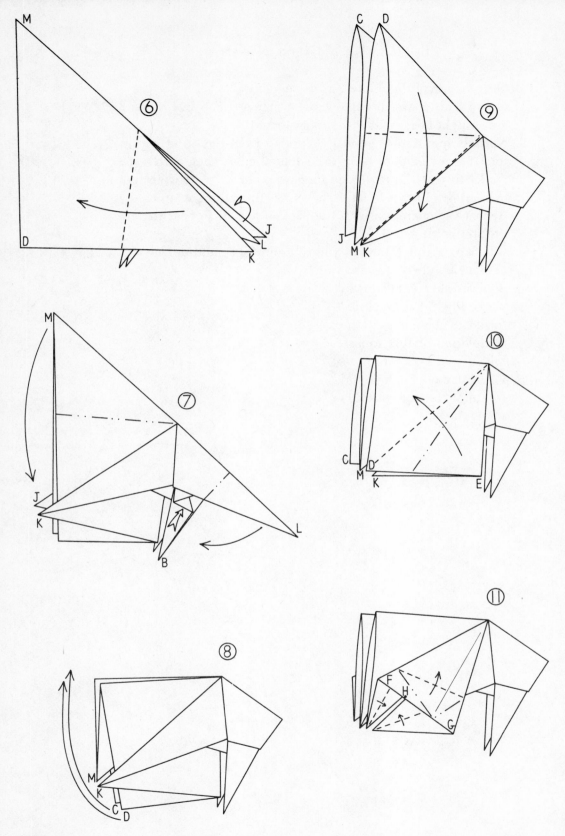

6. Swing flap K to the left as far as it will go. Repeat behind with flap J.
7. Reverse-fold flap M down so that its tip touches the tips of J and K. Reverse-fold flap L into the model. Push the paper at the top of flap B up into the model; repeat behind.
8. Grasp the tips of flaps C and D and lift them up as far as they will go.
9. Lift flap D and squash-fold it. Repeat behind with flap C.
10. Lift flap E and squash-fold it off-center, so that point H in fig. 11 lies about one-third of the way between corners F and G. Repeat behind.
11. Petal-fold the squashed flap upward. Repeat behind.
12. Hold flap D flat against the table at the spot marked O. Grasp flap K by its very tip and swing it to the right. The flap will automatically assume the position shown in fig. 13. Repeat behind.
13. Form flap K into a sort of rabbit-ear by folding it along the existing creases. Repeat behind.
14. Shorten legs K and B by reverse-folding them. Repeat behind. Swing flap D to the right and flatten the model in a sort of squash fold. Repeat behind. Reverse-fold tail L to bring it into view.
15. Form flap D into a kind of rabbit-ear. Note that the valley fold marked N begins well to the right of the edge of trunk M! Repeat behind.

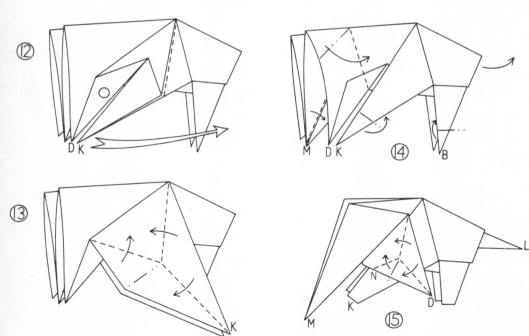

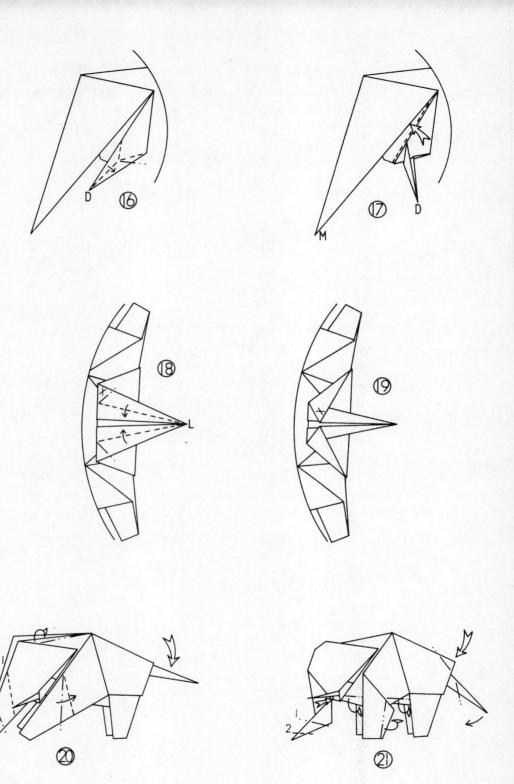

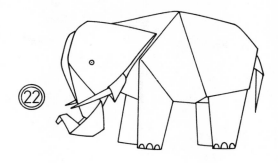

16. Narrow flap D still further by forming it into a rabbit-ear. Repeat behind.

17. Fold the entire tusk-assembly D to the left and tuck it inside trunk M; arrange the tusk so that it remains visible. Repeat behind.

18. This is a bottom view of the tail, with the model spread open. Working from the right, bring the edges together along the center line, flattening the base of the tail into a collar. Watch the spot marked X.

19. The operations of step 18 are shown here completed.

20. Make in order the reverse folds shown on the trunk. Shape the top edge of the neck with a mountain fold; repeat behind. Bring the foreleg into position by forming the valley and mountain folds indicated—the valley fold is made by folding the leg as far toward the tail as possible. Repeat behind. Pull the tail downward and flatten the model.

21. Complete the trunk by making in order the two indicated reverse folds. Narrow the forelegs, belly, and the bottom of the neck with mountain folds. (In order to do this neatly, it is best to separate the two layers of each side of the model.) Cave in the back just above the tail. Reverse-fold the tail downward.

22. An alternative procedure is to reverse-fold flap M not quite down to J and K in step 7, and then form D into a standard rabbit-ear in step 14.

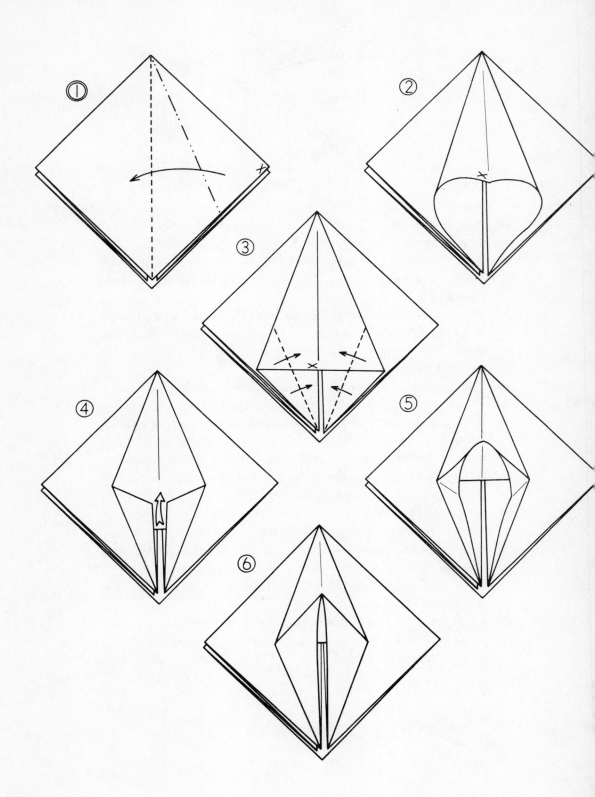

XI. FROG BASE

1. Begin with the Preliminary Fold, page 60. Lift toward you and squash-fold the flap on the right. Watch the spot marked X.
2. The squash fold is shown here in progress.
3. Fold the lower edges of the near flap to the center line.
4. Grasp the covered edge. Pull it up as far as it will go.
5. Now flatten this edge upward into a point, bringing the raw edges together in the center.
6. Repeat steps 1 through 5 on the remaining three flaps.
7. This is the Frog Base, named after the classical Japanese Jumping Frog.

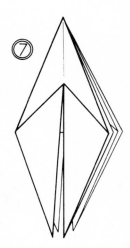

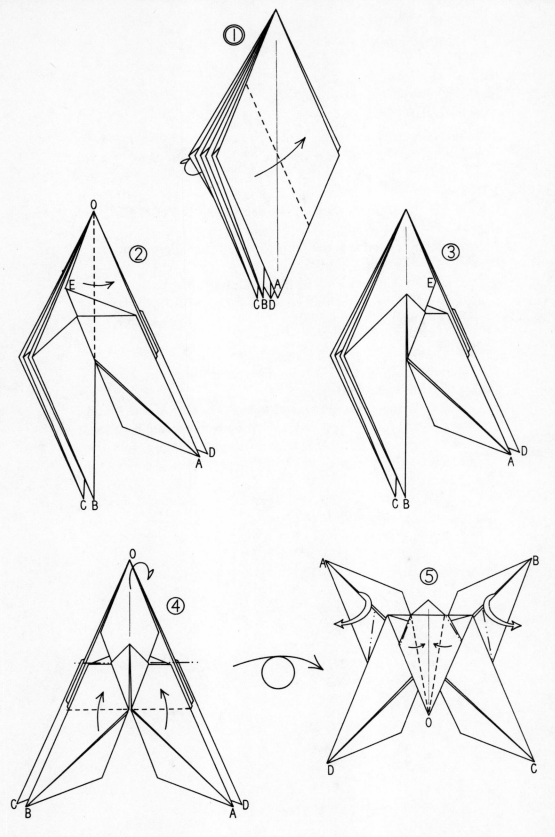

BUTTERFLY
by Jack J. Skillman

Begin with the Frog Base, page 140. Book-fold the front and back flaps of the base to the left.

1. Fold flap A up to the right so that OA in fig. 2 is a straight line. Repeat behind with flap D.

2. Fold flap E to the right. Repeat behind.

3. Repeat these operations (from the beginning through step 2) with flaps B and C, making the right and left halves of the model symmetrical.

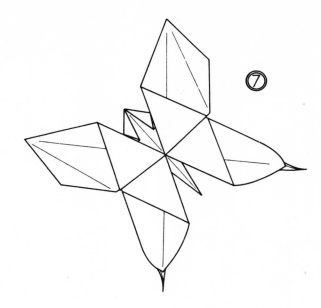

4. Mountain-fold point O down to the rear. Fold wings B and A upward. Turn the model over.

5. Gently pull down the near lower layers of wings A and B and flatten the wings. (These layers must be worked free from the head slightly—see fig. 7.) Working from the bottom, fold the sides of O to the center line and flatten them; a collar will form itself at the top.

6. Form rabbit-ears of wingtips D and C. Mountain-fold the model in half, and turn it over.

7. This model is practical and attractive in tissue paper. See page 71 for a photograph of the Butterfly.

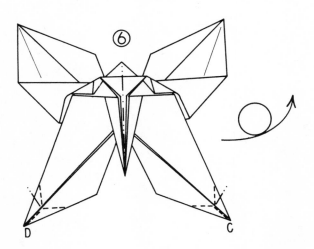

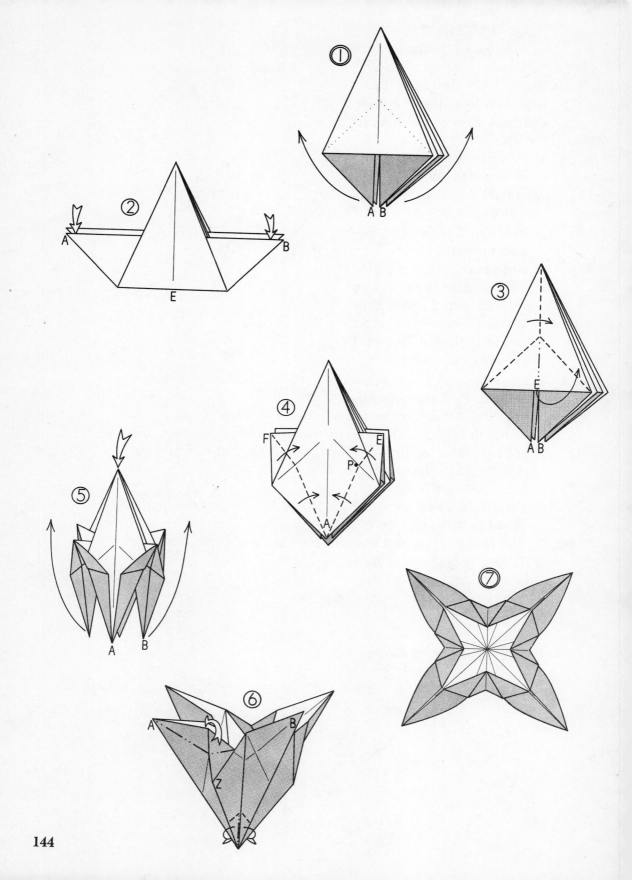

144

FLOWER   *by Philip Shen*

Begin with the Preliminary Fold, page 60, and proceed through step 2 of the Frog Base, page 140. Repeat behind and on the sides. The white side of the paper should face you in fig. 1.

1. Reverse-fold flaps A and B upward so that AB in fig. 2 is a straight line. Repeat behind.

2. Return all flaps to their original positions.

3. Book-fold flap A to the right, lifting E upward. The result is a reverse fold of E analogous to the operations of step 1. Repeat with all remaining flaps. (FE in fig. 4 should be a straight line.)

4. Working from the bottom, fold the lower right edge of flap A to the center line along AP. Then make another valley fold running from P to E. (Note that APE is not a straight line.) Do not flatten the model! Repeat with the left edge of flap A, and then repeat the process with all other flaps.

5. Open out all the flaps completely. Turn the model inside out by pulling the corners of the paper outward while pressing down on the center of the paper. The colored side will now be facing you.

6. While holding flap Z against flap A, mountain-fold the upper edge down into the petal. (No new creases need to be made; the mountain crease already exists.) Repeat with the other side of flap A, and with all remaining flaps. Then form the stem by reverse-folding the bottom of the flower toward yourself. The stem holds the Flower open.

7. This Flower can equally well be made from an equilateral triangle, pentagon, or hexagon.

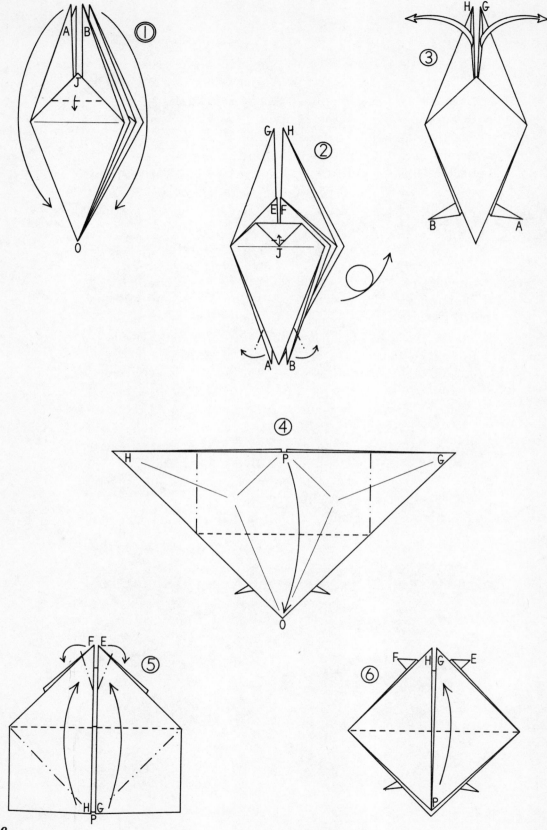

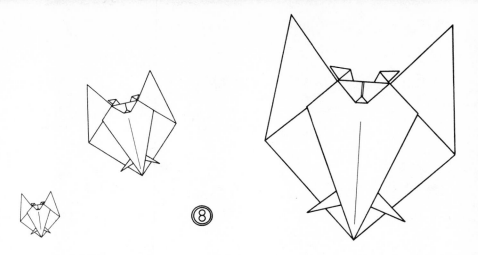

BAT *by Robert Neale*

Turn the Frog Base (page 140) upside down. Arrange J and the three other small flaps so that they point *away* from O.

1. Reverse-fold flaps A and B down as far as they will go. Then fold J downward so that it touches the horizontal crease line.
2. Fold the very tip of nose J upward. Reverse-fold feet A and B outward. (Fig. 8 shows these actions completed.) Turn the model over.
3. Grasp the tips of flaps H and G and pull them outward, opening the near side of the model as shown in fig. 4.
4. Fold the near raw edge down so that point P touches point O. Then flatten the model so that points H and G touch point P.
5. Lift flap H and flatten it upward in a kind of squash fold. Repeat with flap G. Reverse-fold ears F and E outward.
6. Fold P up to the top.
7. Fold P downward so that its tip lies slightly below the horizontal crease line. Pull wings H and G outward and flatten the model. (Note the position of the wings in fig. 8.) Turn the model over.
8. The Bat combines the Frog Base with the Waterbomb Base.

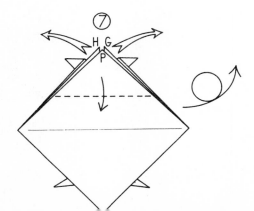

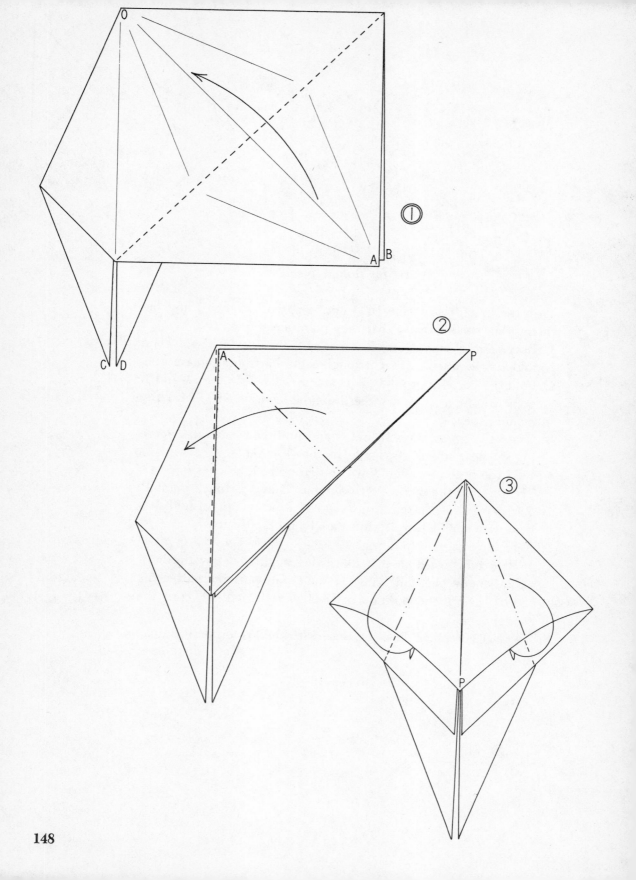

148

HOG *by Samuel Randlett*

Begin with the Frog Base, page 140. Unfold the two front flaps, A and B, into the position shown here.

1. Fold A up to O. Repeat behind with B.
2. Lift flap P and squash-fold it.
3. Tuck in the upper edges of flap P so that they meet inside along the center line.
4. Petal-fold flap P upward.
5. Flaps A and B are snugly wrapped around O. Loosen the tips of A and B, adjusting these flaps into the position shown in fig. 6, and flatten the model. (The distances bracketed in figs. 5 and 6 should be equal.)
6. Tuck the small flaps Y and Z up into the model as indicated. Then fold the model in half and rotate it to the position shown in fig. 7.

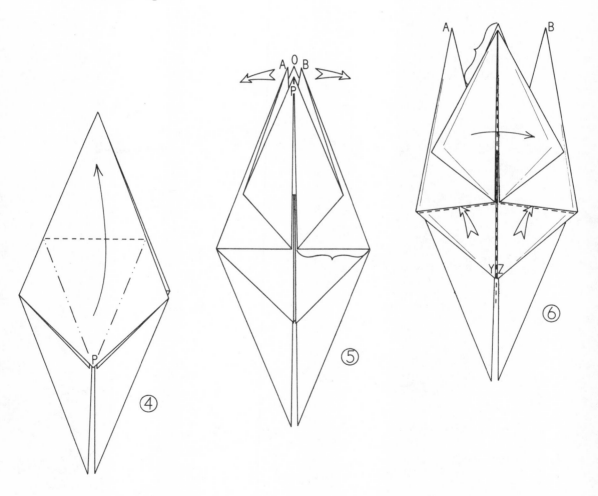

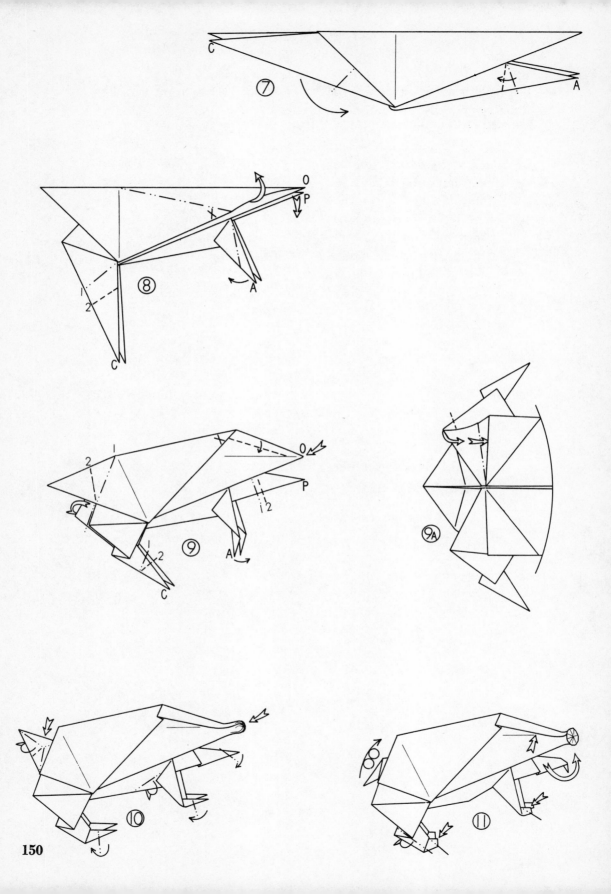

7. Reverse-fold hind leg C downward. Repeat behind. Valley-fold foreleg A to the left and then mountain-fold it to the right. Repeat behind.

8. Make in order the two reverse folds shown on leg C. Reverse-fold leg A to the left. Lift the near edge of the head upward and flatten the model—watch the spot marked X. (During this action, leg C must remain in the same position relative to the near layer of the body; the evenness of the top edges of C will be upset when the model is flattened.) Repeat all of these operations behind. Adjust jaw P downward and flatten the model.

9. Restore the evenness of the top edges of leg C by rolling the excess height into the model. (See fig. 9A.) Make in order the two reverse folds shown on C. Reverse-fold A to the right. Fold down the near top edge of the head. Repeat all of these operations behind. Then make in order the reverse folds shown on the tail and on jaw P. Inflate snout O by pulling on its edges.

9A. The rolling-in action of step 9 is shown here from below. The inner layer is rolled into the pocket that received Y and Z in step 6, and the model is flattened. The action is in progress at the top; at the bottom it is completed.

10. Squash the tail down from the top and petal-fold it up again. Reverse-fold all the hooves to the left. Mountain-fold into the model the edge adjacent to the foreleg; repeat behind. Flatten the snout. Reverse-fold the tip of the lower jaw downward.

11. Twist the tail. Narrow the hind legs. Form cloven hooves by reverse-folding the upper corner of each hoof. Swing the lower jaw up in a counterclockwise direction until its bottom edge is curved and taut. Suggest an eye by pushing the edge of the paper upward; repeat behind.

12. The reverse-folding of A in step 8 may optionally be omitted, and the hooves of the forelegs formed like those of the hind legs in steps 9 through 11. See page 29 for a photograph of the Hog.

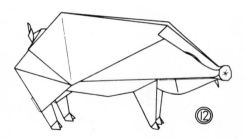

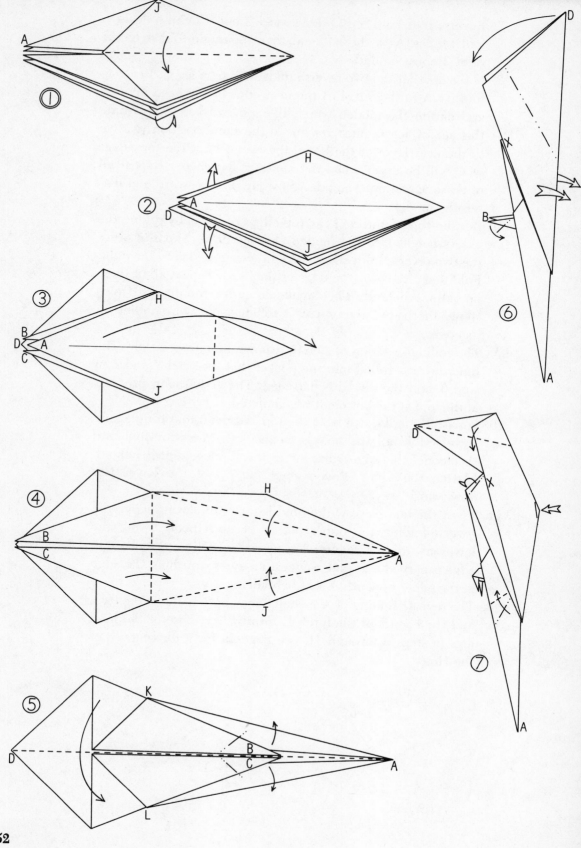

MACAW   *by Adolfo Cerceda*

Begin with the Frog Base, page 140. Rotate the base to the position shown here. The four small flaps should point to the left.

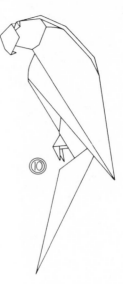

1. Book-fold flap J downward, revealing a smooth surface in front. Repeat behind as shown.
2. Unfold the inner edges of the rear flap D.
3. Hold flaps B and C firmly in place as you pull flap A as far to the right as it will go, "stretching" the small flaps inside. Flatten the base into the position shown in fig. 4.
4. Fold the sides of flap A toward the center line. Fold flaps B and C to the right.
5. Reverse-fold B and C to form legs. Fold the entire model in half and rotate it to the position shown in fig. 6.
6. Reverse-fold B down to form a foot. Repeat behind. Pull the entire outer layer of flap D to the right, adjusting the creases on the inside of the model; watch the spot marked X. Flatten the model. Then reverse-fold the top of flap D to the left.
7. Fold the near surface of flap D in half. Repeat behind. Crimp tail A to the left. Mountain-fold the top of the breast. Repeat behind. Round the back by sinking the point indicated by the hollow arrow.
8. Make in order the numbered reverse folds.
9. Complete the beak by unfolding its inner layers. Lift and squash-fold the eyes. Shape the head with the tiny folds indicated.
10. Pull the legs of the completed Macaw to the left, place the bird on your finger, and release the legs. The spring tension of the legs will hold the Macaw in place.

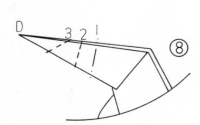

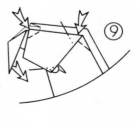

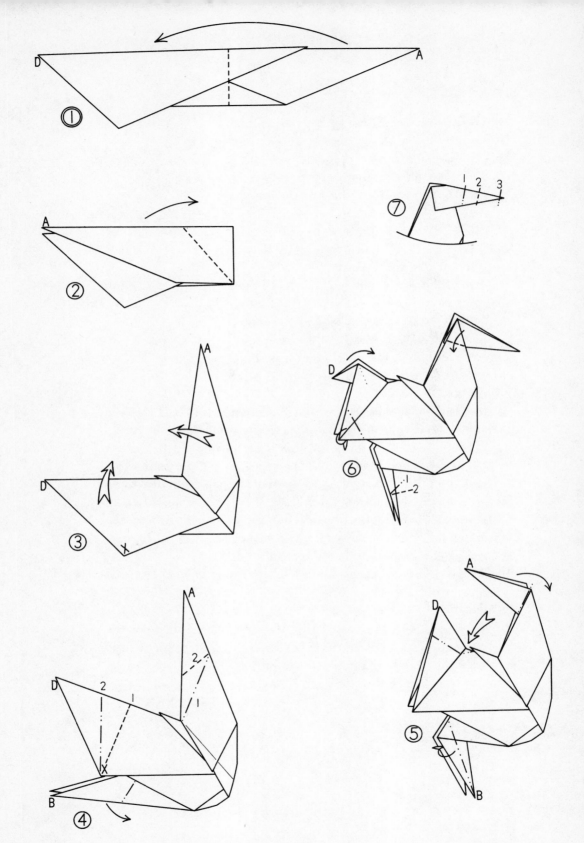

154

HEN   *by Adolfo Cerceda*

Proceed through step 3 of the Macaw, page 152. Fold the model in half.

1. Reverse-fold A to the left so that it touches point D.
2. Reverse-fold flap A up and to the right.
3. Pull flap D upward clockwise, and flap A to the left counter-clockwise, so that the lower right corner of the model will stretch itself into a curve. (Note that flap B remains in place during this operation—see fig. 4.) Watch the spot marked X.
4. Reverse-fold flap B downward. Repeat behind. Make in order the reverse folds shown on flaps D and A.
5. Reverse-fold flap A to the right to begin formation of the head. Sink the top edge of flap D down into the model. Narrow the legs.
6. Reverse-fold tail D up to the right. Mountain-fold the lower left corner of the tail area into the model; repeat behind. Make the two indicated reverse folds in each of the legs to form the feet. Fold the front side of the head downward; repeat behind.
7. Form the beak by making in order the three reverse folds shown.
8. See page 81 for a photograph of the Hen.

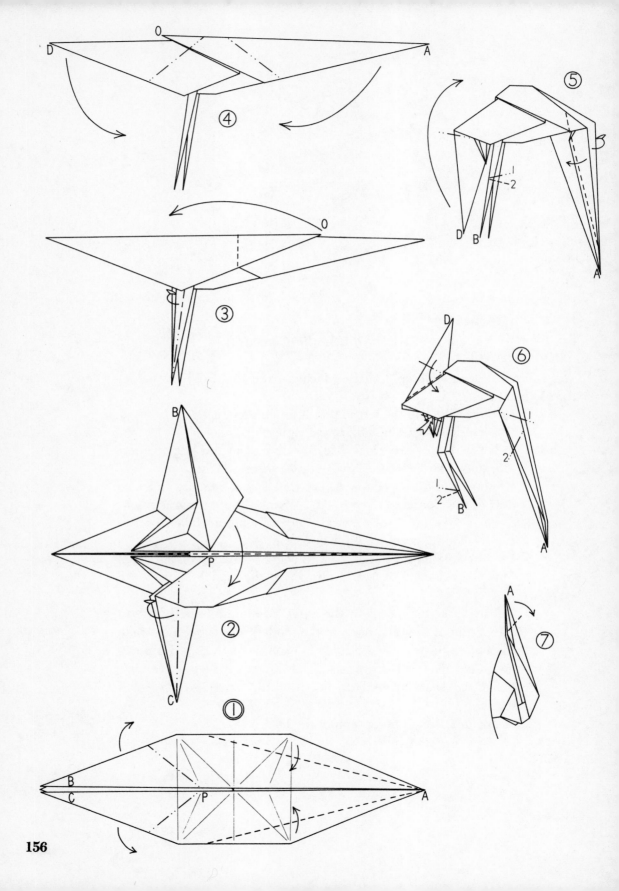

FLAMINGO *by Adolfo Cerceda*

Begin with the Frog Base and proceed through step 3 of the Macaw, page 152, without pulling out the edges of flap D.

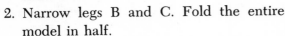

1. Fold the edges of flap A toward the center line. Reverse-fold flaps B and C—note the position of point P! A collar will form itself inside each flap as the model is flattened. In fig. 2, flap B has been opened to show this collar.

2. Narrow legs B and C. Fold the entire model in half.

3. Narrow the legs again. (To narrow the outer layer of the leg, the collar must be adjusted slightly.) Reverse-fold flap O to the left as far as it will go.

4. Reverse-fold flaps D and A downward.

5. Reverse-fold flap D upward. Form in both legs the two reverse folds shown on leg B. Fold the front surface of neck A approximately in half—note that the crease does not touch point A—and repeat behind.

6. Crimp D down around the body. Tuck up into the body the small triangular points indicated by the hollow arrow. Form each foot by making in order the two reverse folds shown on flap B. Note that the two reverse folds shown on flap A are of the same type.

7. Reverse-fold the tip of flap A down to form the head.

8. This is a close-up view of the head. Open its inner layers downward.

9. Make in order the three reverse folds shown.

10. Crimp the beak downward. Then make a crimp in the neck so that the entire head and the top of the neck are tilted slightly downward.

11. The Flamingo will stand. See page 40 for a photograph.

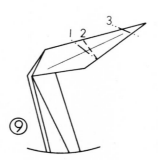

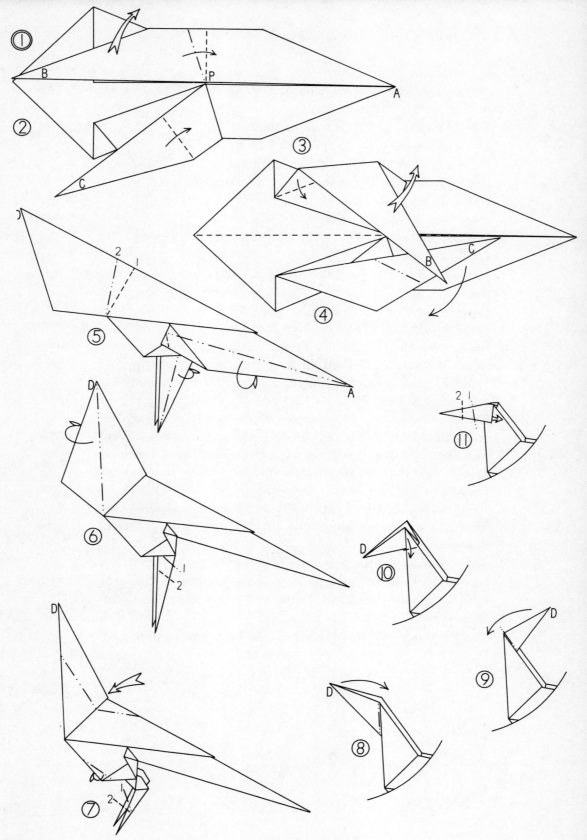

158

PHEASANT *by Adolfo Cerceda*

Begin with the Frog Base and proceed through step 3 of the Macaw, page 152.

1. Swing flap B counterclockwise, pivoting it at point P, and flatten it into position of flap C in fig. 2. The mountain and valley creases will form themselves when flap B is flattened. Repeat with the other flap.
2. Fold flap C as indicated. Repeat with the other flap.
3. Swing flap B counterclockwise and flatten it into the position of flap C in fig. 4. Repeat with the other flap.
4. Reverse-fold flap C downward. Repeat with flap B. Fold the model in half.
5. Make in order the two reverse folds shown in flap D. Working from the right, narrow tail A by tucking its bottom edges up inside as far as possible. Narrow the legs similarly.
6. Tuck the left edges of flap D as far inside as possible. Form in each leg the two reverse folds shown.
7. Sink the upper edge of flap D down into the model. Form in each leg the two reverse folds shown. Mountain-fold the lower edge up into the model as indicated; repeat behind.
8. Reverse-fold flap D to the right.
9. Reverse-fold flap D back to the left.
10. Fold the near surface of flap D downward. Repeat behind.
11. Make in order the two reverse folds shown on the head. Pull the inner right edge of the head out slightly and flatten the model; repeat behind.
12. See page 48 for a photograph of the Pheasant.

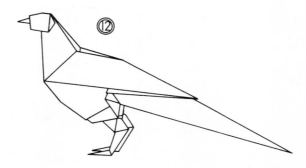

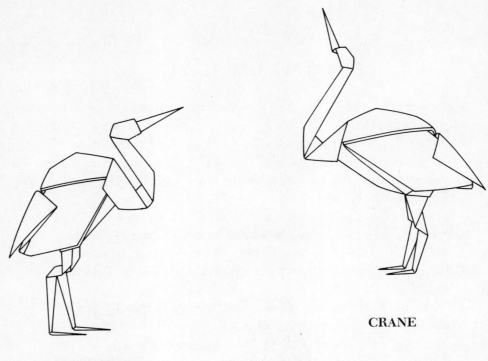

CRANE

WHITE HERON

THREE BIRDS *by Adolfo Cerceda*

The White Heron and Crane are made from the Flamingo, page 156, by varying the folding of the neck, head, and legs. The Parakeet combines the body of the Pheasant, page 158, with the head of the Macaw, page 152.

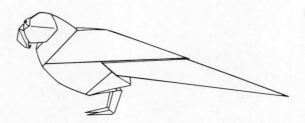

PARAKEET

MACAW and RHINOCEROS
by ADOLFO CERCEDA. In-
structions for the MACAW
appear on *page 152*. The RHI-
NOCEROS is folded from a
single uncut BLINTZ BIRD
BASE.

ROBERT HARBIN

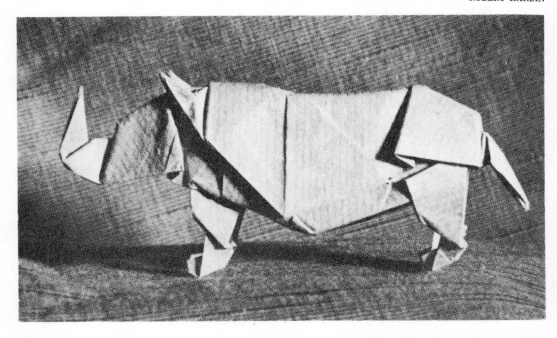

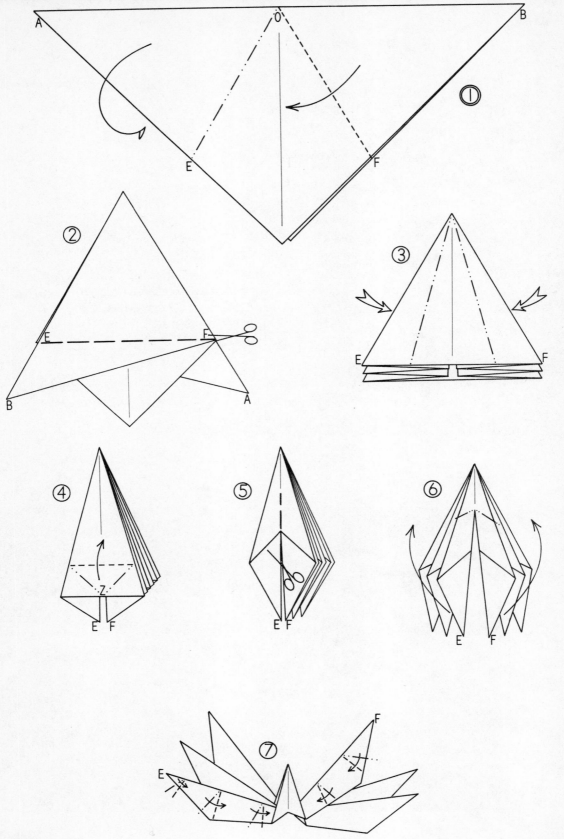

XIII. FROG BASE: HEXAGONAL SHEET

PALM TREE *by Ligia Montoya*

Begin with a square of thin paper folded in half diagonally.

1. Mountain-fold A and valley-fold B so that angles AOE, EOF, and FOB are equal.
2. Cut from E to F through the entire thickness of the model. Arrange the resulting hexagon in the manner of the Waterbomb Base (page 166), as indicated here in fig. 3.
3. Reverse-fold flaps E and F so that their edges touch the center line. Repeat behind and on the sides. Measure the distance from E to F and make a note of it.
4. Petal-fold Z upward. Repeat with all flaps.
5. Slit along the center line as shown. Repeat with all flaps.
6. Reverse-fold flaps E and F upward. Repeat with all flaps.
7. Crimp all the palm fronds as shown. Make each frond different.

The trunk begins with a rectangle of heavy paper twice as long as EF in fig. 3; its width should be one-fifth of its length. Fig. A shows the rectangle folded in half.

A. Fold the trunk in half again.
B. Reverse-fold the trunk back and forth as shown; continue this process almost to the bottom of the trunk.
C. Spread the halves of end H to act as a foundation for the tree, which will stand if a thumbtack is pushed through H. Make a point of end G.
D. Insert the trunk into the fronds. (H is shown here in opened position, tacked down.)
E. The Palm Tree is indispensable for tropical scenes—see pages ii and 40.

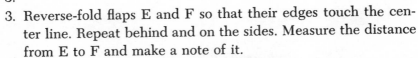

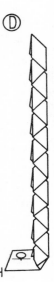

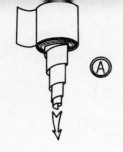

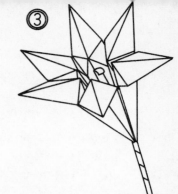

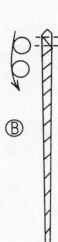

LILY *by Ligia Montoya*

Proceed through step 4 of the Palm Tree fronds, page 162.

1. Unfold the base, turning it inside out by pushing down on point O.
2. Fold all six of the small flaps Z down inside the model as far as they will go. No new creases are needed.
3. Make a small hole in the bottom of the blossom to admit the stem.

Roll a long strip of paper into a coil.

A. Grasp the center of the coil and pull it down to form a tube.
B. Twist the tube to make it as tight as possible. Then flatten the upper end and roll it downward. Insert the stem into the blossom of the Lily and pull it down through the tiny hole.
C. Folding the long flaps instead of the short flaps down inside the blossom in step 2 produces another of Miss Montoya's flowers, not shown here.

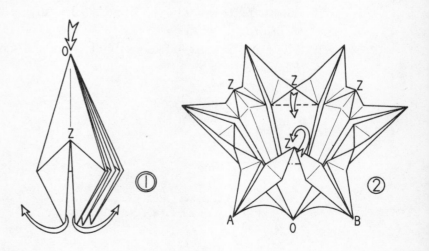

164

CARDINAL by GEORGE RHOADS, *page 170.*

EASTER EGGS by JOHN M. NORDQUIST, *page 167,* with a RABBIT by NEAL ELIAS. The RABBIT is folded from an uncut BIRD BASE; it begins with fig. 3 of the OPERA SINGER, *page 90,* and is closely related to Mr. Elias' LION, *page 92.*

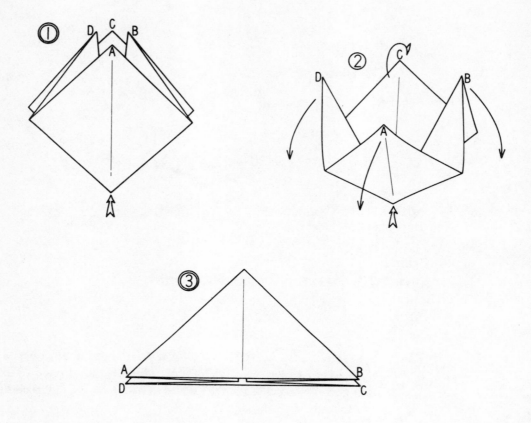

XIV. WATERBOMB BASE

1. Hold the Preliminary Fold with its four corners pointing up. Pull these corners outward and down while pushing up on the center of the paper. This will turn the Preliminary Fold inside out.
2. The action of step 1 is shown here in progress. No new creases are made.
3. The Waterbomb Base is complete.

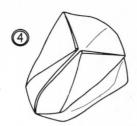

④

EASTER EGG *by John M. Nordquist*

1. Fold points A and B of the Waterbomb Base, page 166, up to the top. Repeat behind.
2. Fold points E and F to the center line at the indicated angle. Repeat behind.
3. Tuck flaps A and B down into the pockets immediately below them. Repeat behind. Inflate the Easter Egg by blowing into the hole at the bottom.
4. The Easter Egg looks festive when made from patterned paper.

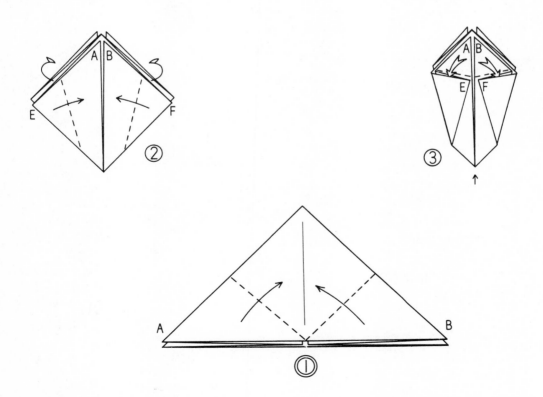

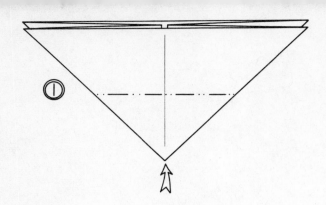

①

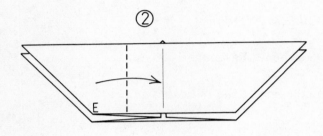

②

E

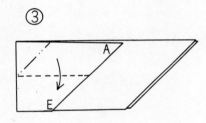

③

A

E

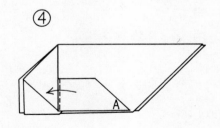

④

A

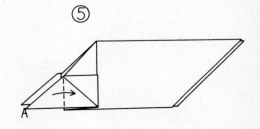

⑤

A

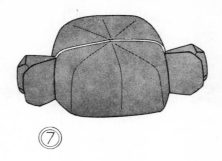

⑦

MATADOR'S HAT   *by Florence Temko*

Begin with a Waterbomb Base, page 166, turned upside down.

1. Sink point O up into the model so that it touches the top edges.
2. Fold point E to the right so that it touches the center line. Repeat behind.
3. Fold the upper edge of flap A down to the bottom and flatten the model. (A sort of collar will form itself at the left as the model is flattened.) Repeat behind.
4. Fold flap A to the left. Repeat behind.
5. Fold flap A to the right. Repeat behind. Then perform steps 2 through 5 on the right side of the model.
6. Round off the corners of the hat's "ears" with valley folds. Then open out the hat from beneath. Fig. 6 shows the hat from the side.
7. The Matador's Hat is shown here from the front.

⑥

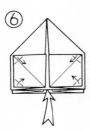

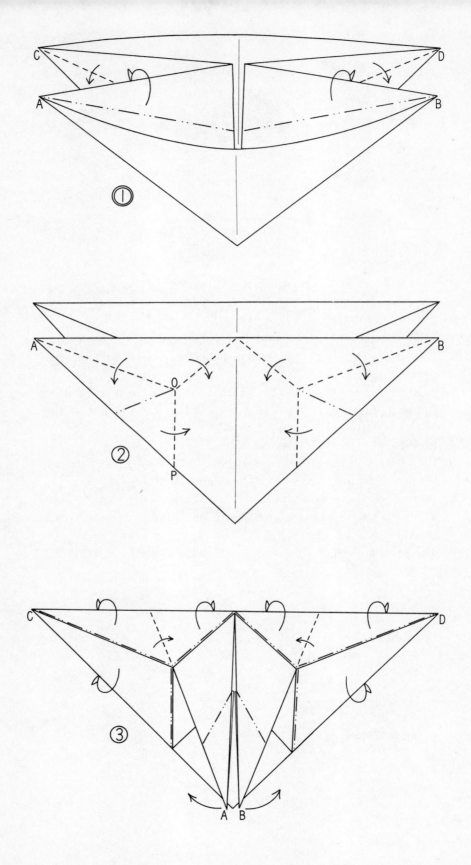

CARDINAL *by George Rhoads*

Use paper colored on both sides. Begin with the Waterbomb Base, page 166. Turn the base upside down.

1. Fold down the raw edge that runs from A to C so that it lies along the folded edge below. Repeat with the edge running from B to D.
2. Form flap A into a rabbit-ear. This is a normal rabbit-ear except that crease OP runs straight up and down. Repeat with flap B.
3. Reverse-fold flaps A and B outward to form the legs. Then mountain-fold flaps C and D into the rabbit-ear configurations shown.
4. Narrow legs A and B. Fold the entire model in half.
5. Narrow the near side of tail E, tucking both layers inside the model and leaving point Z in place. Repeat behind. Reverse-fold F down to form the beak.
6. George Rhoads paints the Cardinal's beak and feet yellow, and adds eyes for realism. See page 165 for a photograph.

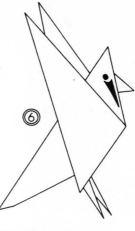

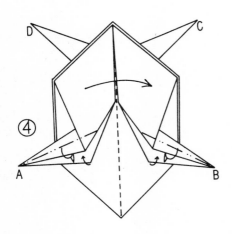

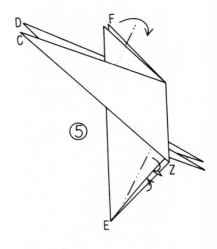

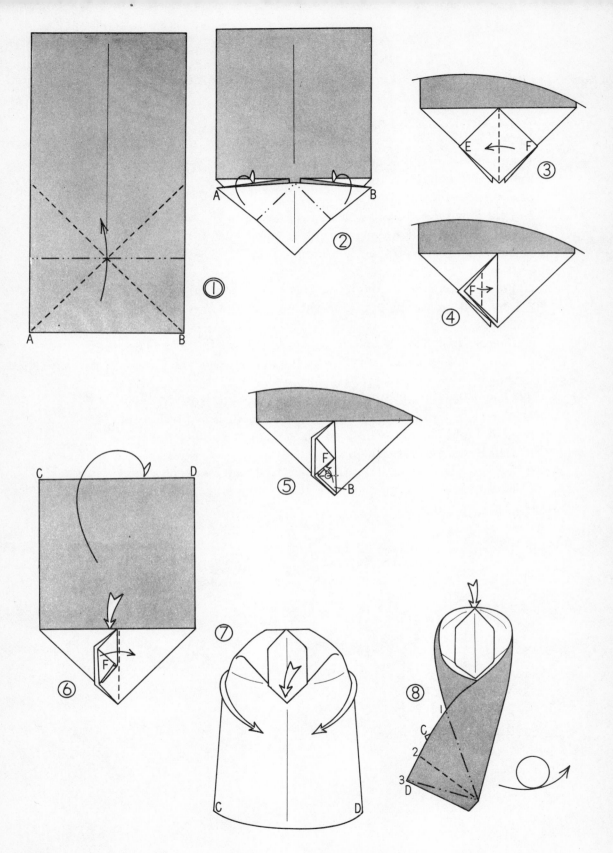

172

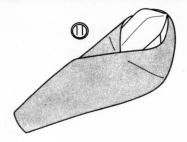

BABY *by Robert Neale*

1. Begin with a two-by-one rectangle. Form the bottom half into a Waterbomb Base.
2. Mountain-fold flaps A and B down to the bottom.
3. Book-fold flap F to the right.
4. Fold point F to the right. Repeat behind with flap E.
5. Fold flap B up so that its tip touches point F. Then tuck the resulting flap up into the pocket on the bottom edge of F. Repeat behind with flap E.
6. Book-fold F to the right. Place the fingers of your right hand into the large pocket indicated by the hollow arrow, and with your left hand pull edge CD to the rear and down to the bottom.
7. Push with your thumbs in the middle of the model as you pull the edges of the paper from the back around to the front. Do this gently to avoid tearing the paper. Bring the right edge over the left to begin formation of the blanket.
8. Hollow out the head from the back. Pleat the blanket back and forth with the mountain and valley folds indicated. Turn the model over.
9. The hollow in the back of the head can be seen here. Fold the tip of the blanket toward the head.
10. This is a side view of the figure. Turn it so that the face is visible.
11. See Robert Neale's Joseph and Mary figures on pages 82 to 84.

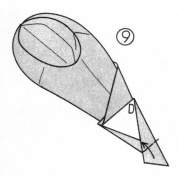

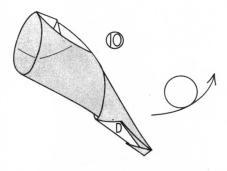

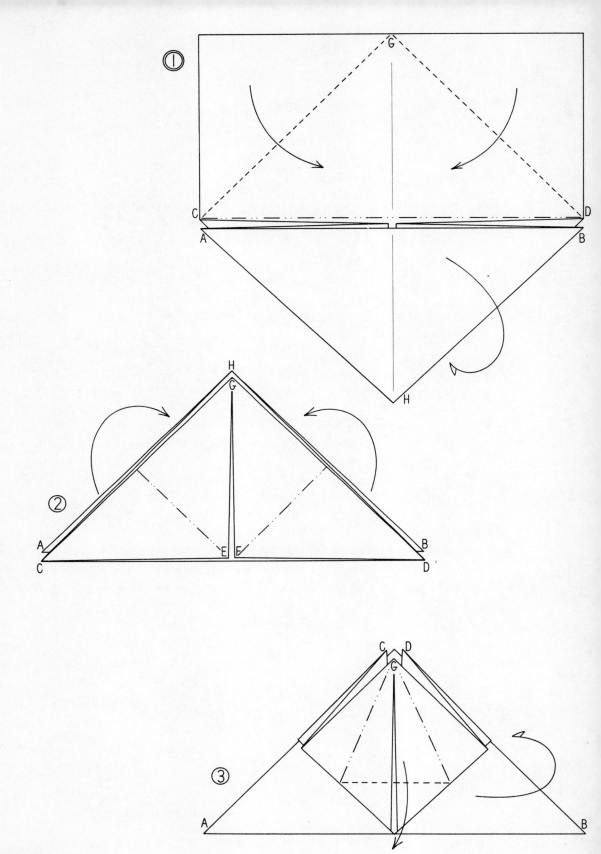

ANGEL *by Neal Elias*

Use paper colored on both sides. Form the bottom square of a two-by-three rectangle into an upside-down Waterbomb Base. (AB is the width of the rectangle.)

1. Fold EG and FG down to the center line. Then mountain-fold the lower portion of the model up to the rear along line CD.
2. Reverse-fold C and D up to the top.
3. Petal-fold flap G downward. Swing flap B behind the model as far as possible, so that it lies in back of flap A.
4. Reverse-fold J and K inward.
5. Fold the entire front construction in half, leaving flaps A and B where they are.
6. Mountain-fold flap Y into the model as far as possible. Repeat behind. Completely unfold the nearest single layer of flap G. Repeat behind.

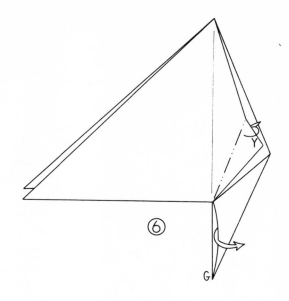

⑥

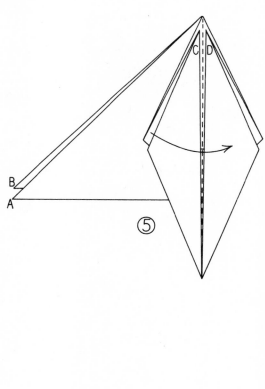

⑤

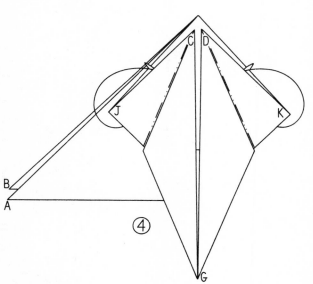

④

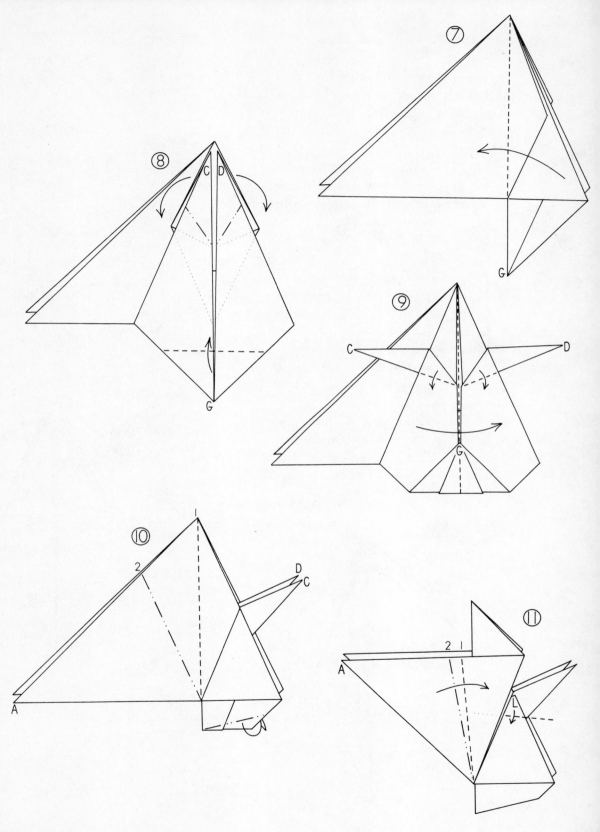

7. Fold the entire front half of flap G to the left.

8. Fold the tip of flap G upward. Reverse-fold flaps C and D. (The X-ray view shows the inside of the model.)

9. Fold arms C and D downward. Then fold the entire front construction in half.

10. Valley- and mountain-fold wing A in the indicated order. Repeat behind. Then mountain-fold the bottom of the robe up into the model. Repeat behind.

11. Valley- and mountain-fold wing A as shown. Repeat behind. Fold area L downward. Repeat behind.

12. Shape the top of the wing with mountain folds as indicated; the valley folds form themselves as the model is flattened. Watch the spot marked X. Make in order the two reverse folds shown on the arm. Mountain-fold the right edge of the robe inward. Repeat all of these operations behind.

13. Reverse-fold the tip of G. Then crimp the hood downward.

14. The front and back halves of the Angel's robe may be locked together by tucking the back half under the front right edge.

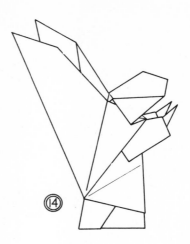

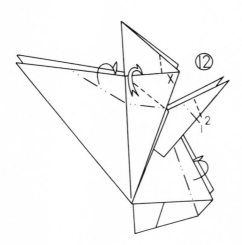

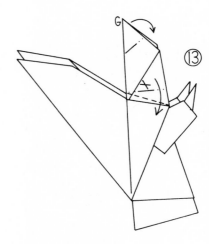

CONTRIBUTORS

ADOLFO CERCEDA, a resident of Chicago, is a native of Argentina. Mr. Cerceda is a master entertainer who has toured the world as a knife thrower and bull-whip expert. He has presented rope acts professionally; he is a skilled stage hypnotist and magician; and he is currently presenting his demonstrations of paper folding throughout the country. Mr. Cerceda, who is the art editor of *The Origamian* and author of two origami books, prefers models that solve some technical or aesthetic problem. He never releases a figure that does not satisfy him completely—"If it does not convince me, I do not believe that it will convince anyone"—and his models, whether simple boxes or intricate animals from multiple bases, are of uniform excellence.

Crane, 160

Flamingo, 156

Hen, 154

Macaw, 152

Parakeet, 160

Pheasant, 158

Rhinoceros, 161

Sofa, 26

White Heron, 160

NEAL ELIAS lives with his wife and their two daughters near Cleveland, Ohio, where he is employed by the Nickle Plate Railroad. Mr. Elias has written a book on card magic, a field in which he is well known for his creative work, and he is a frequent contributor to magic journals. Since 1960, when he began working seriously in origami, Mr. Elias has devised well over three hundred figures, many of them displaying a strong sense of humor. It is his practice to decide first on a basic fold, then on a particular subject to be folded. Mr. Elias's hobbies include, in addition to magic and origami, the raising of Japanese miniature trees.

Angel, 174

Boy on a Dolphin, 76

Indian, 30

José Greco, 110

Lion, 92

Opera Singer, 90

Rabbit, 165

Shoe, 20

Spider Monkey, 116

ROBERT HARBIN is England's foremost professional magician. Mr. Harbin has written several books on conjuring and paper crafts, and he is the author of two fine works on paper folding: *Paper Magic* and *Secrets of Origami* "I find origami a relaxing, stimulating, and challenging hobby. It fascinates me and gives me great pleasure, and I would like it to do the same for all who become interested." Mr. Harbin's many television demonstrations in England and Bermuda have done much to popularize the art. Accident plays little part in Mr. Harbin's creative work; he decides on a subject, and then explores every possible base in pursuit of his goal.

Man in a Boat, 16

LIGIA MONTOYA is a resident of Buenos Aires. She was born in Argentina and educated there and in Spain. By common acclaim, Miss Montoya is the first lady of creative origami. "Dr. Solórzano says that he folds 'scientifically' whereas the Japanese fold 'artistically'—I myself stand midway between these positions. I play with the paper until I vaguely see a model. Or I see the model first and then try to find the most adequate base from which to fold it. Sometimes it happens that I see the figure, explore the bases in an effort to make it, and in the process discover a quite different and unexpected model."

Ape, 120	Mouse, 122
Housefly, 62	Palm Tree, 162
Leaf, 106	Stork, 32
Lily, 164	Swan, 50

ROBERT NEALE, born in 1929, is a Protestant minister who teaches at Union Theological Seminary in New York. His avocations include card tricks, string games, and tangrams; he is interested professionally in the psychology of play. "I began folding paper in 1958. I became acquainted in 1959 with Lillian Oppenheimer and her collection of folds, books, and paperfolders. In that year I created the first and best of my models, the Thurber Dog. For the most part my discoveries of new bases or folds are quite accidental; my attempts to reach a set goal deliberately end usually in frustration or an entirely different outcome than planned. The best models are folded from a single uncut square; their construction is simple and their lines are clean. The complicated folds may be clever and realistic, but simple models may possess a style that is true art. This style is my objective and occasional joy."

Baby, 172	Mary, 84
Bat, 146	Thurber Dog, 42
Joseph, 82	Whale, 44

JOHN M. NORDQUIST was born in 1904 in Portland, Oregon. He holds an M.S. degree from the University of Oklahoma, and has done advanced study at the California Institute of Technology. Since 1933 Mr. Nordquist has been an assistant at the Seismological Laboratory in Pasadena, California. "My intense interest in paper folding began in 1957, when I learned a number of new folds from a Japanese seismologist who encouraged me to invent new models. My forte appears to be finding new variations on folds from bases originated by others. I have participated in origami exhibits in Pasadena and New York; a few of my original figures appear in Randlett's *The Art of Origami*."

Easter Egg, 167	Ornament, 18
Icicles, 118	Super Susan, 38

SAMUEL RANDLETT, born in 1930, is a native of Milwaukee and a graduate of Northwestern University. Mr. Randlett is a piano teacher currently on leave from the faculty of Fisk University for advanced study. His hobbies include magic, and he has contributed several articles to periodicals in the field. Mr. Randlett's creative work began in 1959 when he encountered Harbin's *Paper Magic*. Many of his models appear in his book, *The Art of Origami*. Mr. Randlett has preferred the improvisatory method of devising figures: he works intensively with a basic fold, applying to it various technical procedures until the possibility of a model presents itself.

Apartheid, 98	Parrot, 25
Eagle, 22	Purses, 99
Hog, 148	Songbird, 24
Owl and Pussycat, 46	

GEORGE RHOADS, born in Chicago in 1926, is a graduate of the University of Chicago. He is an artist—his paintings have been shown in New York, Chicago, and Paris—and a serious amateur graphologist and astrologer. Mr. Rhoads has illustrated several children's books. Along with housepainting and carpentry, he does painting of the *trompe l'oeil* variety professionally. Mr. Rhoads' own romantic, ungeometrical origami style was developed at a time when other folders were working exclusively in a classical idiom. "I think of the thing, usually an animal, that I want to make, and then go to work on the paper. I have discovered new principles and new bases this way. The beauty of origami is the beauty of economy. Everything is put to good use—no idle points are hidden away, there is no clumsy thickness, no complex device that could be simplified. I consider my Elephant to be the most perfect of my foldings with regard to economy of means."

Bug, 130	Fardel Bearer, 74
Bull, 72	Giraffe, 112
Cardinal, 170	Piglet, 28
Elephant, 134	Tyrannosaurus rex, 128

FREDRIC G. ROHM, born in 1907, is a graduate of the University of Pennsylvania. He is Chief Experimental Engineer for the Lycoming Division of the AVCO Corporation in Montoursville, Pennsylvania; he holds a number of internal combustion engine patents. Mr. Rohm has been a professional musician and a semiprofessional magician, as well as an amateur ham radio enthusiast. His hobbies include science fiction and puzzles. As a boy, Mr. Rohm learned to fold the Lovers' Knot and the Waterbomb. When he stopped smoking in 1959, he began to fold these figures to keep his hands occupied. Then, without knowledge that origami existed outside of these two models, he proceeded to invent the art and carry it to a high level of sophistication. By the time Mr. Rohm contacted other American folders in 1961, he had produced a large and impressive menagerie of figures.

Halloween Cat, 86	Star Flowers, 132
Skunk, 56	Turkey, 78
Squirrel, 52	Whistler's Mother, 102

PHILIP SHEN, who is of Chinese ancestry, was born in Manila in the Philippines. Mr. Shen is a member of the faculty of Chung Chi College in Hong Kong; he holds a Ph.D. in Christian Theology from the Divinity School of the University of Chicago. He has taught origami extensively, and has organized its terminology and basic procedures into a system well adapted to teaching purposes. "In Hong Kong there seems to be very little interest in paper folding as a Chinese folk art; only the most elementary books and models can be found. Origami, like any other art, must be constantly renewed by creative experimentation—and the recent Western achievements may, in a sense, give paper folding back to China."

Flower, 144

JACK J. SKILLMAN was born in 1915 in Terre Haute, Indiana. He has taught crafts and horticulture, and is currently a civil service employee of the Chicago Board of Health. Mr. Skillman folded paper intensively for thirty years before contacting Lillian Oppenheimer in 1959. Working in isolation, he invented many of the most advanced procedures of geometrical origami, by logical variation of basic principles "In judging any model my standard is *finish*, and I never release or accept a fold that does not seem to be completed in the best possible way."

Butterfly, 142	Japanese Lantern, 108

E. D. SULLIVAN: "A third of a century ago I was a student assistant in the Bell Telephone Laboratories. Today I am a laboratory supervisor in the Boeing Company in Seattle, Washington. Between these way stations I have been salesman, professional gambler, inventor, textile designer, advertising salesman, artist, soldier, officer, sign salesman, television installer, and analog computer expert. Most of my effort in origami has been directed toward models that do something, and some of them are by-products of a continuing analysis of motion in paper figures. The fascination of creativity lies chiefly in the happy marriage of deliberation and chance."

Kissing Penguins, 68   Togetherness, 96
Table, 100

FLORENCE TEMKO, who lives in New Shrewsbury, New Jersey, is the author of *Kirigami, the Creative Art of Papercutting*. Mrs. Temko has demonstrated origami on television both in America and in England; she is best known as a lecturer who teaches her audiences, large or small, to fold origami models. Mrs. Temko's library of step-by-step folds for six hundred traditional and modern figures is unique. "I love the challenge of creating new models for particular occasions."

Hatchet, 14   Matador's Hat, 168

HARRY WEISS is the chief press officer for the United States Department of Commerce, where he has served for seventeen years under six Secretaries. Mr. Weiss was born in Newark, New Jersey, in 1915; he is a graduate of Antioch College. He received his newspaper training as a reporter for the Cleveland *Plain Dealer*. Mr.. Weiss is married and the father of three children. "I have been interested in paper folding and amateur magic since my childhood. I am also an incorrigible writer of bad verse. My intense interest in origami started when I saw some figures made by a Catholic priest. This Philippino Churchman had been using the hobby in his work with patients in a New York hospital. He introduced me to Harbin's *Paper Magic* and I've been at it since."

Fawn, 70   Tumbling Chan, 64

BIBLIOGRAPHY

Arnstein, Bennett. *Origami Polyhedra: How to Make Three-Dimensional Geo-metric Models*. New York: Exposition Press, 1968. Origami bases from squares, triangles, and pentagons are joined with tape to form strikingly attractive ornamental constructions.

Cerceda, Adolfo. *Folding Money*. Chicago: Magic, Inc., 1963. This thirty-six page booklet, illustrated with one hundred drawings, is devoted exclusively to figures folded from dollar bills.

Guy, Mick. *Origami 'One'*. Birmingham: Malcolm Peters (Thorp Street), 1971. Eleven good models of intermediate difficulty by nine different folders, clearly and accurately presented.

Harbin, Robert. *Secrets of Origami: The Japanese Art of Paper Folding*. London: Octopus Books Limited, 1971. One hundred and fifty models are explained by fourteen hundred drawings and seventy photographs. The leading folders of the world have contributed original models to this wonderful anthology, which contains also a large section of traditional folds. This book and *The Best of Origami* are mutually complementary.

———. *Paper Magic*. London: John Maxfield Limited, 1971. This fine book, which contains over a hundred models, is so organized as to be especially helpful in the study of origami procedures.

———. *Origami: The Art of Paper-Folding*. London: Hodder Paperbacks, 1969.

———. *More Origami: The Art of Paper-Folding No. 2*. London: Hodder, 1971.

Three important paperbacks devoted largely to recent creations.

———. *Origami Compendium No. 1*. London: John Maxfield Limited, 1970. An excellent collection of twenty figures, some traditional and others original with Robert Harbin. Paper is included in the kit.

Kenneway, Eric. *Simple Origami*. Leicester: The Dryad Press, 1970. About a dozen fine new models splendidly illustrated by the author.

———. *Origami in Action*. Leicester: The Dryad Press, 1972. Another good booklet: ten action models which spin, flap, pop, tip, and inflate.

Nakamura, Eiji. *Flying Origami: Origami from Pure Fun to True Science*. San Francisco: Japan Publications, Inc., 1972. Twenty-eight new airplanes from rectangles of one proportion in three different sizes.

Nakano, Dokuohtei. *Correspondence Course of Origami*. Dokuohtei Nakano Origami Institute, 32-6, Kamikitazawa 3–chome, Setagaya-ku, Tokyo, 156, Japan. The twelve lessons of this beautifully drawn course are in English; paper, photographs, finished and half-finished models are included. Some 250 of the author's birds, animals, reptiles, insects, and human figures are developed with gradually increasing complexity from a system of basic folds. This impressive course is strongly recommended to the serious origami enthusiast as a worthwhile investment.

Palacios, Vicente. *Papirogami*. Barcelona: Editorial Miguel A. Salvatella, 1972. About fifty models are presented, along with many logically related variants. The models stem largely from the Spanish tradition, but there are contributions from England and the United States as well; all are carefully drawn. An English translation of the general introductory essay is provided. This book belongs in every origami library.

Randlett, Samuel. *The Art of Origami: Paper Folding, Traditional and Modern*. London: Faber and Faber, 1963. Fifty-seven models, many of them by the author, are explained in five hundred and forty-one line drawings and forty-eight photographs by Jean Randlett. The format, organization, and conventions of illustration are the same as those of the present volume. Essays on origami history, teaching, and creation are included.

————. *Bunny Bill*. Chicago: Magic, Inc., 1964. Robert Neale's rabbit that pops out of a hat, folded from a single dollar bill.

————. *The Flapping Bird. An Origami Monthly*. A periodical presenting new works by the finest creative folders, published by Jay Marshall, Bookseller, 5082 North Lincoln Avenue, Chicago, Illinois 60625, U.S.A.

————. *Folding Money, Volume Two*. Chicago: Magic, Inc., 1968. The alphabet from dollar bills, with origami by Neal Elias and Robert Neale.

Sakade, Florence. *Origami*, volumes 1, 2, and 3. Rutland, Vermont: Charles E. Tuttle Company, 1957, 1958, 1959. Good teaching material from the Japanese tradition—each volume contains about sixteen models.

Sakoda, James Minoru. *Modern Origami*. New York: Simon and Schuster, 1969. Fifty original models in the author's highly individual style.

Soong, Maying. *The Art of Chinese Paper Folding for Young and Old*. New York: Harcourt, Brace and Co., 1948. Easy models—the Chinese tradition.

Takahama, Toshie. *Creative Life With Creative Origami*. Makō-sha Publishing Co., Ltd., 14–6, Hongo 4–chome, Bunkyo-ku, Tokyo, Japan. A good solid book of 186 pages, notable especially for two dozen pages of color photographs of origami uses and displays. Nicely illustrated models of moderate difficulty, with each model titled in English.

Uchiyama, Koshio. *Origami*. Kokudosha, Takata Toyokawa Cho, Bunkyo-ku, Tokyo, Japan. This large work, published in 1962, deals in part with cut-and-fold origami, but there are many excellent uncut models, including some outstanding furniture. The thorough chart of crease patterns in basic folds deserves careful study.

————. *Origami Asobi* (Origami Play). Kokudosha, Takata Toyokawa Cho, Bunkyo-ku, Tokyo, Japan. This colorful little book, published in 1967, contains over two dozen fresh and imaginative models by the author—see, for example, the pleated Turkey. The figures are of intermediate difficulty.

van Breda, Aart. *Paper Folding and Modelling*. London: Faber and Faber, 1965. Good simple models appropriate for teaching.

Yoshizawa, Akira. *Origami Dokuhon I* (Creative Origami). Kamakura Shobo Co., Ltd., 21 Ichigaya-Sanaicho, Shinjuku-ku, Tokyo, Japan. The 1967 edition of this great work contains an English translation. There are more than sixty models, each a masterpiece. Mr. Yoshizawa has produced several other books of his magnificent figures; these volumes may had be directly from Akira Yoshizawa, P.O. Box 3, Ogikubo, Tokyo, Japan.

An origami organization:
The Secretary
British Origami Society
33, Fleming Road
Quinton, Birmingham, 32

An origami periodical:
The Origamian
The Origami Center
71 West 11th Street
New York, N.Y. 10011

INDEX

(page numbers in italics indicate a photograph)

ACTION MODELS:
Kissing Penguins, 68
Owl and Pussycat, 46
Tumbling Chan, 64
Whistler's Mother, 102
ANIMALS:
Ape, 120, *63*
Bat, 146
Bull, 72
Cat, Halloween, 86
Dog, Thurber, 42
Elephant, 134, *ii*
Fawn, 70
Giraffe, 112, *ii*
Hog, 148, *28*
Lion, 92, *ii*
Monkey, Spider, 116, *40*
Mouse, 122
Piglet, 28
Pussycat, Owl and, 46
Rabbit, *165*
Rhinoceros, *161*
Skunk, 56
Squirrel, 52
Tyrannosaurus rex, 128, *125*
BASIC FOLDS:
Bird Base, 66
    multiple, 108
    stretched, 96
    unusual shapes, 118
Blintz Bird Base, 126
Diamond Base, 41
Fish Base, 49
Frog Base, 140
    stretched, 152
    hexagonal sheet, 162
Preliminary Fold, 60
Waterbomb Base, 166
BIRDS:
Apartheid, 98
Cardinal, 170, *165*
Crane, 160
Eagle, 22
Flamingo, 156, *40*
Hen, 154, *81*
Heron, White, 160
Macaw, 152, *161*
Owl and Pussycat, 46
Parakeet, 160
Parrot, 25, *40*
Penguins, Kissing, 68
Pheasant, 158, *48*
Songbird, 24
Stork, 32
Swan, 50
Togetherness, 96
Turkey, 78

FISH:
Dolphin, Boy on a, 76, *48*
Whale, 44
HUMAN FIGURES:
Angel, 174
Baby, 172, *85*
Boy on a Dolphin, 76, *48*
Fardel Bearer, 74, *69*
Greco, José, 110, *73*
Indian, 30
Joseph, 82, *85*
Man in Boat, 17
Mary, 84, *85*
Opera Singer, 90
Tumbling Chan, 64
Whistler's Mother, 102
INSECTS:
Bug, 130, *69*
Butterfly, 142, *71*
Housefly, 62
OBJECTS:
Boat, Man in a, 17
Easter Egg, 167, *165*
Hat, Matador's, 168
Hatchet, 14
Icicles, 118, *109*
Lantern, Japanese, 108
Lazy Susan, 36
Ornament, 18, *109*
Purses, 99
Shoe, 20
Sofa, 26
Super Susan, 38
Table, 100
PLANTS:
Flower, 144
Leaf, 106
Lily, 164
Palm Tree, 162, *ii*, *40*
Star Flowers, 132
PROCEDURES:
book fold, 19
crimp, 19
Lovers' Knot move, 10
mountain fold, 15
petal fold, 11
rabbit-ear, 18
reverse fold, 9
sinking a point, 10
squash fold, 11
valley fold, 15